The State of The Union

For more information on our Presidential Project, or if you would like for Morgan James Publishing to consider publishing your manuscript visit MorganJamesPublishing.com.

ISBN: 0-9758570-3-7

RONALD REAGAN

The State of The Union

A tribute to Ronald Reagan

David L. Hancock

2004

THE STATE OF THE UNION

"The President shall from time to time give to Congress information of the State of the Union and recommend to their Consideration such measures as he shall judge necessary and expedient."

—Article II, Sec. 3, U.S. Constitution

THE STATE OF THE UNION

This Book is dedicated to promoting the legacy of President Ronald Reagan, to fulfilling the vision of his life's work and to ensure that America's future remains bright. The Ronald Reagan Presidential Library is dedicated to the President's enduring message of freedom. To realize President Reagan's dreams for our generation and generations to come, a Memorial Fund has been established to benefit his Library in Simi Valley, California.

A portion of the proceeds are being donated to that fund.

To make a gift to the Ronald Reagan Memorial Fund, please visit www.RonaldReaganMemorial.com.

THE STATE OF THE UNION

Table of Contents

THE STATE OF THE UNION

Foreword

Ronald Reagan believed that everything happened for a reason, and that we can trust in God's purposes. He believed that people are basically good. He had no tolerance for bigotry or injustice. Above all, he believed in the courage and triumph of free men and in the capacity of the American people to overcome any obstacle.

President Reagan took those convictions to the White House in 1981, and he departed eight years later with achievements that have endured. With bold, persistent action, he restored the confidence of our nation, strengthened the spirit of free enterprise, challenged and shamed an oppressive empire, and inspired millions with his conviction and moral courage.

As he showed what a President should be, he also showed us what a man should be. Ronald Reagan carried himself with a decency and attention to the small kindnesses that also define a good life. He was a courtly, gentle, and considerate man, never known to slight or embarrass others. From the Oval Office, he took time to answer letters from schoolchildren and grandmothers and countless strangers curious about life in the White House.

Ronald Reagan deeply loved the United States of America. And that love was returned. Tens of thousands of mourners stood in line in California and in Washington, D.C. to pay their final respects. There were 21-gun salutes and dignified processions, and home-made memorials at a funeral home in Santa Monica.

Our country is stronger and our world is freer for the brave leadership of this modest son of America. Ronald Reagan always told us that for America, our best was yet to come. We know that is true for him, too. His work is done. And now, as President George W. Bush said, "a shining city awaits him".

Ronald Reagan

At the end of his two terms in office, Ronald Reagan viewed with satisfaction the achievements of his innovative program known as the Reagan Revolution, which aimed to reinvigorate the American people and reduce their reliance upon Government. He felt he had fulfilled his campaign pledge of 1980 to restore "the great, confident roar of American progress and growth and optimism."

On February 6, 1911, Ronald Wilson Reagan was born to Nelle and John Reagan in Tampico, Illinois. He attended high school in nearby Dixon and then worked his way through Eureka College. There, he studied economics and sociology, played on the football team, and acted in school plays. Upon graduation, he became a radio sports announcer. A screen test in 1937 won him a contract in Hollywood. During the next two decades he appeared in 53 films.

From his first marriage to actress Jane Wyman, he had two children, Maureen and Michael. Maureen passed away in 2001. In 1952 he married Nancy Davis, who was also an actress, and they had two children, Patricia Ann and Ronald Prescott.

As president of the Screen Actors Guild, Reagan became embroiled in disputes over the issue of

Communism in the film industry; his political views shifted from liberal to conservative. He toured the country as a television host, becoming a spokesman for conservatism. In 1966 he was elected Governor of California by a margin of a million votes; he was re-elected in 1970.

Ronald Reagan won the Republican Presidential nomination in 1980 and chose as his running mate former Texas Congressman and United Nations Ambassador George Bush. Voters troubled by inflation and by the year-long confinement of Americans in Iran swept the Republican ticket into office. Reagan won 489 electoral votes to 49 for President Jimmy Carter.

On January 20, 1981, Reagan took office. Only 69 days later he was shot by a would-be assassin, but quickly recovered and returned to duty. His grace and wit during the dangerous incident caused his popularity to soar.

Dealing skillfully with Congress, Reagan obtained legislation to stimulate economic growth, curb inflation, increase employment, and strengthen national defense. He embarked upon a course of cutting taxes and Government expenditures, refusing to deviate from it when the strengthening of defense forces led to a large deficit.

A renewal of national self-confidence by 1984 helped Reagan and Bush win a second term with an unprecedented number of electoral votes. Their victory turned away Democratic challengers Walter F. Mondale and Geraldine Ferraro.

In 1986 Reagan obtained an overhaul of the income tax code, which eliminated many deductions and exempted millions of people with low incomes. At the end of his administration, the Nation was enjoying its longest recorded period of peacetime prosperity without recession or depression.

In foreign policy, Reagan sought to achieve "peace through strength." During his two terms he increased defense spending 35 percent, but sought to improve relations with the Soviet Union. In dramatic meetings with Soviet leader Mikhail Gorbachev, he negotiated a treaty that would eliminate intermediate-range nuclear missiles. Reagan declared war against international terrorism, sending American bombers against Libya after evidence came out that Libya was involved in an attack on American soldiers in a West Berlin nightclub.

By ordering naval escorts in the Persian Gulf, he maintained the free flow of oil during the Iran-Iraq war. In keeping with the Reagan Doctrine, he gave support to anti-Communist insurgencies in Central America, Asia, and Africa.

Overall, the Reagan years saw a restoration of prosperity, and the goal of peace through strength seemed to be within grasp.

THE STATE OF THE UNION

The State of the Union Address, a Tradition Since 1790

The State of the Union is one of only a few presidential speeches that are televised live in prime time on all major U.S. networks. This has elevated its prominence enormously compared to earlier times. For over a hundred years, it wasn't even delivered in person by the president. Instead, it was sent to Congress as a written message.

The tradition goes back to 1790 when George Washington, the first president of the United States, delivered his "Annual Message," as it was known then, as required by the Constitution. Article II, Section III states that the president shall "from time to time give to the Congress information of the State of the Union, and recommend to their consideration such measures as he shall judge necessary and expedient." These "innocuous phrases conferred on the American president what has become, after vicissitudes, a basic tool in his management of Congress and a potent instrument of national leadership," writes the historian Arthur Schlesinger, Jr., in his book, "The State of the Union Messages of the Presidents."

Washington and his successor, John Adams, delivered addresses in person surrounded by much pomp and ceremony, as was the custom under the rule of the English kings before independence. But the nation's third president, Thomas Jefferson, felt that such elaborate displays ill befit the new democratic republic. He derided the practice as a "speech from the throne," and instead delivered a written message rather than appearing in person. Jefferson's influence was such that for more than a century thereafter, the Annual Message would be written and sent to Congress rather than delivered in person.

In the early decades, most State of the Union messages were laundry lists of bills the president wanted the Congress to enact -- often reflective of the tenor of the times and the practical problems involved in building the young American nation. Until the Civil War (1861-65), the speeches also often dealt with internal threats to the union, reflecting a major concern of the Founding Fathers. During this time, the annual reports "were, understandably, preoccupied with how tenuous were the ties of national union," writes Wayne Fields in his book, "Union of Words: A History of Presidential Eloquence."

In addition, the speeches also dealt with the international situation and America's place in the world, not least in this hemisphere. A prime example is President James Monroe's Annual Message to Congress in 1823 opposing European intervention in the Americas. Speaking directly to the European powers of the day, Monroe wrote, "We owe it, therefore, to candor and to the amicable relations existing between the United States and those powers to declare that we should consider any attempt on their part to extend their system to any portion of this hemisphere as dangerous to our peace and safety." In the decades that followed, the Monroe Doctrine often would be invoked by presidents to indicate America's determination to keep this hemisphere master of its own destiny.

In particularly turbulent periods, some presidents used the State of the Union address as a vehicle to express their view of great issues then at stake and their vision of the road ahead -- speaking not just to lawmakers but to their fellow citizens, to the world at large, and, in some instances, to the ages. During the crisis that, more than any other, threatened the very existence of the American union -- the Civil War -- President Abraham Lincoln wrote perhaps the most eloquent and memorable of all presidential messages sent to Congress.

When the speech was delivered on December 1, 1862, it was clear that the state of the union was not good, the outcome of the war still uncertain, the defeat of the Confederate rebellion by no means a foregone conclusion. But Lincoln rose to the occasion. Characteristically, his words went to the heart of the struggle then engulfing the nation -- framing for all Americans, and for the world, the essential choice to be made.

"The dogmas of the quiet past are inadequate to the stormy present," he wrote. "The occasion is piled high with difficulty and we must rise to the occasion. As our case is new, so we must think anew and act anew. We must disenthrall ourselves, and then we shall save our country. Fellow citizens, we cannot escape history. We of this Congress and this administration will be remembered in spite of ourselves." He added: "In giving freedom to the slave, we assure freedom to the free -- honorable alike in what we give and what we preserve. We shall nobly save or meanly lose the last best hope of earth. Other means may succeed. This could not fail. The way is plain, peaceful, generous, just -- a way which if followed the world will forever applaud and God must forever bless." It was, wrote historian Arthur Schlesinger, "the highest eloquence of all Annual Messages ... profound and beautiful."

In 1913, Woodrow Wilson revived the practice of delivering the Annual Message in person that had been pioneered by Washington and Adams more than a century earlier. "A president is likely to read his own message rather better than a clerk would," he quipped. The two-term president, famous for championing the League of Nations, the precursor organization to the United Nations, used the occasion to deliver a wide-ranging speech, mostly centered on domestic policy.

Wilson's decision to appear in person was prescient. The United States was on the eve of an electronic mass media revolution that would soon bring presidents into the homes of Americans via radio, and, after World War II, via television.

Although Wilson's words were not heard by most Americans, his moving image became familiar to them through silent newsreels.

With the election of Franklin Delano Roosevelt (FDR) as president in 1932, Americans would become accustomed to hearing their presidents on radio as well as seeing them -

- and now hearing them -- on the newsreels at the movies. One of his most enduring speeches was the Annual Message he delivered in 1941. With war raging across Europe, he set forth his famous Four Freedoms.

"In the future days," he said, "which we seek to make secure, we look forward to a world founded upon four essential freedoms. The first is freedom of speech and expression, everywhere in the world. The second is freedom of every person to worship God in his own way, everywhere in the world. The third is freedom from want ... everywhere in the world. The fourth is freedom from fear ... anywhere in the world." Later that year, after the attack on Pearl Harbor on December 7, Roosevelt addressed a special joint session of Congress to ask for a declaration of war against Japan.

In 1945, the Annual Message formally became known as the State of the Union address. It also was about to become a television as well as radio staple as sales of television sets skyrocketed in the years after World War II. In recognition of the power of television to deliver the president's words to a huge audience, President Lyndon Johnson shifted the time of the address from the traditional midday to evening when more viewers would be watching.

"And now, in 1965, we begin a new quest for union," Johnson said in his first State of the Union address that year. He detailed an expansive vision of a "Great Society," in which poverty would be eliminated and the civil rights of all Americans would be protected. Although his reports are not considered eloquent by most historians, they are reflective of Johnson's sweeping agenda and the liberal ethos then dominant in American society. His speeches followed in the tradition of a generation of progressivism in American life -- from Roosevelt's New Deal beginning in the early 1930s to John F. Kennedy's New Frontier of the early 1960s.

A very different direction was charted by Ronald Reagan in his first State of the Union address delivered in 1982. Reagan used the occasion to detail an unambiguous conservative agenda not only in domestic affairs, but also foreign policy. "Together, after 50 years of taking power away from the hands of the people in their states and local communities," he said, "we have started returning power and resources to them." Reagan articulated a new interpretation of limited federal power in the U.S. system of government, the influence of which was enduring. Even Bill Clinton, a president with very different views from those of Reagan, famously said in one of his State of the Union addresses, "the era of big government is over."

Although Reagan devoted most of his remarks to domestic policy in his 1982 speech, he did not neglect relations overseas, particularly with the Soviet Union. "In the last decade," he said, "while we sought the moderation of Soviet power through a policy of restraint and accommodation, the Soviets engaged in an unrelenting buildup of their military forces. The protection of our national security has required that we undertake a substantial program to enhance our military forces." He added: "A recognition of what the Soviet empire is about is the starting point."

The broadcast of the State of the Union address on television, particularly when it was moved to prime time, has changed the fundamental nature of the message, according to political observers. "As the audience has changed from inside the [Washington] Beltway to outside," says Paul C. Light, a prominent political scientist with the Brookings Institution, "the State of the Union has changed from a sometimes windy policy address to a major campaign event," one, it might be added, in which the primary audience is now the American voter, and the wider audience overseas, rather than the American lawmaker.

This was certainly true when President George W. Bush delivered his State of the Union address on January 29, 2002. Both domestic and overseas observers will be looking to the president for an indication of how the events of September 11 have reshaped the U.S. domestic and foreign policy agenda.

THE STATE OF THE UNION

First Inaugural Address of Ronald Reagan

TUESDAY, JANUARY 20, 1981

Senator Hatfield, Mr. Chief Justice, Mr. President, Vice President Bush, Vice President Mondale, Senator Baker, Speaker O'Neill, Reverend Moomaw, and my fellow citizens: To a few of us here today, this is a solemn and most momentous occasion; and yet, in the history of our Nation, it is a commonplace occurrence. The orderly transfer of authority as called for in the Constitution routinely takes place as it has for almost two centuries and few of us stop to think how unique we really are. In the eyes of many in the world, this every-4-year ceremony we accept as normal is nothing less than a miracle.

Mr. President, I want our fellow citizens to know how much you did to carry on this tradition. By your gracious cooperation in the transition process, you have shown a watching world that we are a united people pledged to maintaining a political system which guarantees individual liberty to a greater degree than any other, and I thank you and your people for all your help in maintaining the continuity which is the bulwark of our Republic.

The business of our nation goes forward. These United States are confronted with an economic affliction of great proportions. We suffer from the longest and one of the worst sustained inflations in our national history. It distorts our economic decisions, penalizes thrift, and crushes the struggling young and the fixed- income elderly alike. It threatens to shatter the lives of millions of our people.

Idle industries have cast workers into unemployment, causing human misery and personal indignity. Those who do work are denied a fair return for their labor by a tax system which penalizes successful achievement and keeps us from maintaining full productivity.

But great as our tax burden is, it has not kept pace with public spending. For decades, we have piled deficit upon deficit, mortgaging our future and our children's future for the temporary convenience of the present. To continue this long trend is to guarantee tremendous social, cultural, political, and economic upheavals.

You and I, as individuals, can, by borrowing, live beyond our means, but for only a limited period of time. Why, then, should we think that collectively, as a nation, we are not bound by that same limitation?

We must act today in order to preserve tomorrow. And let there be no misunderstanding--we are going to begin to act, beginning today.

The economic ills we suffer have come upon us over several decades. They will not go away in days, weeks, or months, but they will go away. They will go away because we, as Americans, have the capacity now, as we have had in the past, to do whatever needs to be done to preserve this last and greatest bastion of freedom.

In this present crisis, government is not the solution to our problem.

From time to time, we have been tempted to believe that society has become too complex to be managed by self-rule, that government by an elite group is superior to government for, by, and of the people. But if no one among us is capable of governing himself, then who among us has the capacity to govern someone else? All of us together, in and out of government, must bear the burden. The solutions we seek must be equitable, with no one group singled out to pay a higher price.

We hear much of special interest groups. Our concern must be for a special interest group that has been too long neglected. It knows no sectional boundaries or ethnic and racial divisions, and it crosses political party lines. It is made up of men and women who raise our food, patrol our streets, man our mines and our factories, teach our children, keep our homes, and heal us when we are sick-- professionals, industrialists, shopkeepers, clerks, cabbies, and truck drivers. They are, in short, "We the people," this breed called Americans.

Well, this administration's objective will be a healthy, vigorous, growing economy that provides equal opportunity for all Americans, with no barriers born of bigotry or discrimination. Putting America back to work means putting all Americans back to work. Ending inflation means freeing all Americans from the terror of runaway living costs. All must share in the productive work of this "new beginning" and all must share in the bounty of a revived economy. With the idealism and fair play which are the core of our system and our strength, we can have a strong and prosperous America at peace with itself and the world.

So, as we begin, let us take inventory. We are a nation that has a government--not the other way around. And this makes us special among the nations of the Earth. Our Government has no power except that granted it by the people. It is time to check and reverse the growth of government which shows signs of having grown beyond the consent of the governed.

It is my intention to curb the size and influence of the Federal establishment and to demand recognition of the distinction between the powers granted to the Federal Government and those reserved to the States or to the people. All of us need to be reminded that the Federal Government did not create the States; the States created the Federal Government.

Now, so there will be no misunderstanding, it is not my intention to do away with government. It is, rather, to make it work-work with us, not over us; to stand by our side, not ride on our back. Government can and must provide opportunity, not smother it; foster productivity, not stifle it.

If we look to the answer as to why, for so many years, we achieved so much, prospered as no other people on Earth, it was because here, in this land, we unleashed the energy and individual genius of man to a greater extent than has ever been done before. Freedom and the dignity of the individual have been more available and assured here than in any other place on Earth. The price for this freedom at times has been high, but we have never been unwilling to pay that price.

It is no coincidence that our present troubles parallel and are proportionate to the intervention and intrusion in our lives that result from unnecessary and excessive growth of government. It is time for us to realize that we are too great a nation to limit ourselves to small dreams. We are not, as some would have us believe, loomed to an inevitable decline. I do not believe in a fate that will all on us no matter what we do. I do believe in a fate that will fall on us if we do nothing. So, with all the creative energy at our command, let us begin an era of national renewal. Let us renew our determination, our courage, and our strength. And let us renew; our faith and our hope.

We have every right to dream heroic dreams. Those who say that we are in a time when there are no heroes just don't know where to look. You can see heroes every day going in and out of factory gates. Others, a handful in number, produce enough food to feed all of us and then the world beyond. You meet heroes across a counter--and they are on both sides of that counter. There are entrepreneurs with faith in themselves and faith in an idea who create new jobs, new wealth and opportunity. They are individuals and families whose taxes support the Government and whose voluntary gifts support church, charity, culture, art, and education. Their patriotism is quiet but deep. Their values sustain our national life.

I have used the words "they" and "their" in speaking of these heroes. I could say "you" and "your" because I am addressing the heroes of whom I speak--you, the citizens of this blessed land. Your dreams, your hopes, your goals are going to be the dreams, the hopes, and the goals of this administration, so help me God.

We shall reflect the compassion that is so much a part of your makeup. How can we love our country and not love our countrymen, and loving them, reach out a hand when they fall, heal them when they are sick, and provide opportunities to make them self- sufficient so they will be equal in fact and not just in theory?

Can we solve the problems confronting us? Well, the answer is an unequivocal and emphatic "yes." To paraphrase Winston Churchill, I did not take the oath I have just taken with the intention of presiding over the dissolution of the world's strongest economy.

In the days ahead I will propose removing the roadblocks that have slowed our economy and reduced productivity. Steps will be taken aimed at restoring the balance between the various levels of government. Progress may be slow--measured in inches and feet, not miles--but we will progress. Is it time to reawaken this industrial giant, to get government back within its means, and to lighten our punitive tax burden. And these will be our first priorities, and on these principles, there will be no compromise.

On the eve of our struggle for independence a man who might have been one of the greatest among the Founding Fathers, Dr. Joseph Warren, President of the Massachusetts Congress, said to his fellow Americans, "Our country is in danger, but not to be despaired of.... On you depend the fortunes of America. You are to decide the important questions upon which rests the happiness and the liberty of millions yet unborn. Act worthy of yourselves."

Well, I believe we, the Americans of today, are ready to act worthy of ourselves, ready to do what must be done to ensure happiness and liberty for ourselves, our children and our children's children.

And as we renew ourselves here in our own land, we will be seen as having greater strength throughout the world. We will again be the exemplar of freedom and a beacon of hope for those who do not now have freedom.

To those neighbors and allies who share our freedom, we will strengthen our historic ties and assure them of our support and firm commitment. We will match loyalty with loyalty. We will strive for mutually beneficial relations. We will not use our friendship to impose on their sovereignty, for or own sovereignty is not for sale.

As for the enemies of freedom, those who are potential adversaries, they will be reminded that peace is the highest aspiration of the American people. We will negotiate for it, sacrifice for it; we will not surrender for it--now or ever.

Our forbearance should never be misunderstood. Our reluctance for conflict should not be misjudged as a failure of will. When action is required to preserve our national security, we will act. We will maintain sufficient strength to prevail if need be, knowing that if we do so we have the best chance of never having to use that strength.

Above all, we must realize that no arsenal, or no weapon in the arsenals of the world, is so formidable as the will and moral courage of free men and women. It is a weapon our adversaries in today's world do not have. It is a weapon that we as Americans do have. Let that be understood by those who practice terrorism and prey upon their neighbors.

I am told that tens of thousands of prayer meetings are being held on this day, and for that I am deeply grateful. We are a nation under God, and I believe God intended for us to be free. It would be fitting and good, I think, if on each Inauguration Day in future years it should be declared a day of prayer.

This is the first time in history that this ceremony has been held, as you have been told, on this West Front of the Capitol. Standing here, one faces a magnificent vista, opening up on this city's special beauty and history. At the end of this open mall are those shrines to the giants on whose shoulders we stand.

Directly in front of me, the monument to a monumental man: George Washington, Father of our country. A man of humility who came to greatness reluctantly. He led America out of revolutionary victory into infant nationhood. Off to one side, the stately memorial to Thomas Jefferson. The Declaration of Independence flames with his eloquence.

And then beyond the Reflecting Pool the dignified columns of the Lincoln Memorial. Whoever would understand in his heart the meaning of America will find it in the life of Abraham Lincoln.

Beyond those monuments to heroism is the Potomac River, and on the far shore the sloping hills of Arlington National Cemetery with its row on row of simple white markers bearing crosses or Stars of David. They add up to only a tiny fraction of the price that has been paid for our freedom.

Each one of those markers is a monument to the kinds of hero I spoke of earlier. Their lives ended in places called Belleau Wood, The Argonne, Omaha Beach, Salerno and halfway around the world on Guadalcanal, Tarawa, Pork Chop Hill, the Chosin Reservoir, and in a hundred rice paddies and jungles of a place called Vietnam.

Under one such marker lies a young man--Martin Treptow--who left his job in a small town barber shop in 1917 to go to France with the famed Rainbow Division. There, on the western front, he was killed trying to carry a message between battalions under heavy artillery fire.

We are told that on his body was found a diary. On the flyleaf under the heading, "My Pledge," he had written these words: "America must win this war. Therefore, I will work, I will save, I will sacrifice, I will endure, I will fight cheerfully and do my utmost, as if the issue of the whole struggle depended on me alone."

The crisis we are facing today does not require of us the kind of sacrifice that Martin Treptow and so many thousands of others were called upon to make. It does require, however, our best effort, and our willingness to believe in ourselves and to believe in our capacity to perform great deeds; to believe that together, with God's help, we can and will resolve the problems which now confront us.

And, after all, why shouldn't we believe that? We are Americans. God bless you, and thank you.

The State of the Union on January 26, 1982

Mr. Speaker, Mr. President, distinguished Members of the Congress, honored guests, and fellow citizens:

Today marks my first State of the Union address to you, a constitutional duty as old as our Republic itself.

President Washington began this tradition in 1790 after reminding the Nation that the destiny of self-government and the "preservation of the sacred fire of liberty" is "finally staked on the experiment entrusted to the hands of the American people." For our friends in the press, who place a high premium on accuracy, let me say: I did not actually hear George Washington say that. But it is a matter of historic record.

But from this podium, Winston Churchill asked the free world to stand together against the onslaught of aggression. Franklin Delano Roosevelt spoke of a day of infamy and summoned a nation to arms. Douglas MacArthur made an unforgettable farewell to a country he loved and served so well. Dwight Eisenhower reminded us that peace was purchased only at the price of strength. And John F. Kennedy spoke of the burden and glory that is freedom.

When I visited this Chamber last year as a newcomer to Washington, critical of past policies which I believed had failed, I proposed a new spirit of partnership between this

Congress and this administration and between Washington and our State and local governments. In forging this new partnership for America, we could achieve the oldest hopes of our Republic—prosperity for our nation, peace for the world, and the blessings of individual liberty for our children and, someday, for all of humanity.

It's my duty to report to you tonight on the progress that we have made in our relations with other nations, on the foundation we've carefully laid for our economic recovery, and finally, on a bold and spirited initiative that I believe can change the face of American government and make it again the servant of the people.

Seldom have the stakes been higher for America. What we do and say here will make all the difference to autoworkers in Detroit, lumberjacks in the Northwest, steelworkers in Steubenville who are in the unemployment lines; to black teenagers in Newark and Chicago; to hard-pressed farmers and small businessmen; and to millions of everyday Americans who harbor the simple wish of a safe and financially secure future for their children. To understand the state of the Union, we must look not only at where we are and where we're going but where we've been. The situation at this time last year was truly ominous.

The last decade has seen a series of recessions. There was a recession in 1970, in 1974, and again in the spring of 1980. Each time, unemployment increased and inflation soon turned up again. We coined the word "stagflation" to describe this.

Government's response to these recessions was to pump up the money supply and increase spending. In the last 6 months of 1980, as an example, the money supply increased at the fastest rate in postwar history--13 percent. Inflation remained in double digits, and government spending increased at an annual rate of 17 percent. Interest rates reached a staggering 21.5 percent. There were 8 million unemployed.

Late in 1981 we sank into the present recession, largely because continued high interest rates hurt the auto industry and construction. And there was a drop in productivity, and the already high unemployment increased.

This time, however, things are different. We have an economic program in place, completely different from the artificial quick fixes of the past. It calls for a reduction of the rate of increase in government spending, and already that rate has been cut nearly in half. But reduced spending the first and smallest phase of a 3-year tax rate reduction designed to stimulate the economy and create jobs. Already interest rates are down to 15 ¾ percent, but they must still go lower. Inflation is down from 12.4 percent to 8.9, and for the month of December it was running at an annualized rate of 5.2 percent. If we had not acted as we did, things would be far worse for all Americans than they are today. Inflation, taxes, and interest rates would all be higher.

A year ago, Americans' faith in their governmental process was steadily declining. Six out of 10 Americans were saying they were pessimistic about their future. A new kind of defeatism was heard. Some said our domestic problems were uncontrollable, that we had to learn to live with this seemingly endless cycle of high inflation and high unemployment.

There were also pessimistic predictions about the relationship between our administration and this Congress. It was said we could never work together. Well, those predictions were wrong. The record is clear, and I believe that history will remember this as an era of American renewal, remember this administration as an administration of change, and remember this Congress as a Congress of destiny.

Together, we not only cut the increase in government spending nearly in half, we brought about the largest tax reductions and the most sweeping changes in our tax structure since the beginning of this century. And because we indexed future taxes to the rate of inflation, we took away government's built-in profit on inflation and its hidden incentive to grow larger at the expense of American workers.-

Together, after 50 years of taking power away from the hands of the people in their States and local communities, we have started returning power and resources to them.

Together, we have cut the growth of new Federal regulations nearly in half. In 1981 there were 23,000 fewer pages in the Federal Register, which lists new regulations, than there were in 1980. By deregulating oil we've come closer to achieving energy independence and helped bring down the cost of gasoline and heating fuel.

Together, we have created an effective Federal strike force to combat waste and fraud in government. In just 6 months it has saved the taxpayers more than $2 billion, and it's only getting started.

Together we've begun to mobilize the private sector, not to duplicate wasteful and discredited government programs, but to bring thousands of Americans into a volunteer effort to help solve many of America's social problems.

Together we've begun to restore that margin of military safety that ensures peace. Our country's uniform is being worn once again with pride.

Together we have made a New Beginning, but we have only begun.

No one pretends that the way ahead will be easy. In my Inaugural Address last year, I warned that the "ills we suffer have come upon us over several decades. They will not go away in days, weeks, or months, but they will go away . . . because we as Americans have the capacity now, as we've had it in the past, to do whatever needs to be done to preserve this last and greatest bastion of freedom."

The economy will face difficult moments in the months ahead. But the program for economic recovery that is in place will pull the economy out of its slump and put us on the road to prosperity and stable growth by the latter half of this year. And that is why I can report to you tonight that in the near future the state of the Union and the economy will be better—much better—if we summon the strength to continue on the course that we've charted.

And so, the question: If the fundamentals are in place, what now? Well, two things. First, we must understand what's happening at the moment to the economy. Our current problems are not the product of the recovery program that's only just now getting underway, as some would have you believe; they are the inheritance of decades of tax and tax and spend and spend.

Second, because our economic problems are deeply rooted and will not respond to quick political fixes, we must stick to our carefully integrated plan for recovery. That plan is based on four commonsense fundamentals: continued reduction of the growth in Federal spending; preserving the individual and business tax reductions that will stimulate saving and investment; removing unnecessary Federal regulations to spark productivity; and maintaining a healthy dollar and a stable monetary policy, the latter a responsibility of the Federal Reserve System.

The only alternative being offered to this economic program is a return to the policies that gave us a trillion-dollar debt, runaway inflation, runaway interest rates and unemployment. The doubters would have us turn back the clock with tax increases that would offset the personal tax rate reductions already passed by this Congress. Raise present taxes to cut future deficits, they tell us. Well, I don't believe we should buy that argument.

There are too many imponderables for anyone to predict deficits or surpluses several years ahead with any degree of accuracy. The budget in place, when I took office, had been projected as balanced. It turned out to have one of the biggest deficits in history. Another example of the imponderables that can make deficit projections highly questionable—a change of only one percentage point in unemployment can alter a deficit up or down by some $25 billion.

As it now stands, our forecast, which we're required by law to make, will show major deficits starting at less than a hundred billion dollars and declining, but still too high. More important, we're making progress with the three keys to reducing deficits: economic growth, lower interest rates, and spending control. The policies we have in place will reduce the deficit steadily, surely, and in time, completely.

Higher taxes would not mean lower deficits. If they did, how would we explain that tax revenues more than doubled just since 1976; yet in that same 6-year period we ran the largest series of deficits in our history. In 1980 tax revenues increased by $54 billion, and in 1980 we had one of our all-time biggest deficits. Raising taxes won't balance the budget; it will encourage more government spending and less private investment. Raising taxes will slow economic growth, reduce production, and destroy future jobs, making it more difficult for those without jobs to find them and more likely that those who now have jobs could lose them. So, I will not ask you to try to balance the budget on the backs of the American taxpayers.

I will seek no tax increases this year, and I have no intention of retreating from our basic program of tax relief. I promise to bring the American people—to bring their tax rates down and to keep them down, to provide them incentives to rebuild our economy, to save, to invest in America's future. I will stand by my word. Tonight I'm urging the American people: Seize these new opportunities to produce, to save, to invest, and together we'll make this economy a mighty engine of freedom, hope, and prosperity again.

Now, the budget deficit this year will exceed our earlier expectations. The recession did that. It lowered revenues and increased costs. To some extent, we're also victims of our own success. We've brought inflation down faster than we thought we could, and in doing this, we've deprived government of those hidden revenues that occur when inflation pushes people into higher income tax brackets. And the continued high interest rates last year cost the government about $5 billion more than anticipated.

We must cut out more nonessential government spending and rout out more waste, and we will continue our efforts to reduce the number of employees in the Federal work force by 75,000.

The budget plan I submit to you on February 8th will realize major savings by dismantling the Departments of Energy and Education and by eliminating ineffective subsidies for business. We'll continue to redirect our resources to our two highest budget priorities—a strong national defense to keep America free and at peace and a reliable safety net of social programs for those who have contributed and those who are in need.

Contrary to some of the wild charges you may have heard, this administration has not and will not turn its back on America's elderly or America's poor. Under the new budget, funding for social insurance programs will be more than double the amount spent only 6 years ago. But it would be foolish to pretend that these or any programs cannot be made more efficient and economical.

The entitlement programs that make up our safety net for the truly needy have worthy goals and many deserving recipients. We will protect them. But there's only one way to see to it that these programs really help those whom they were designed to help. And that is to bring their spiraling costs under control.

Today we face the absurd situation of a Federal budget with three-quarters of its expenditures routinely referred to as "uncontrollable." And a large part of this goes to entitlement programs.

Committee after committee of this Congress has heard witness after witness describe many of these programs as poorly administered and rife with waste and fraud. Virtually every American who shops in a local supermarket is aware of the daily abuses that take place in the food stamp program, which has grown by 16,000 percent in the last 15 years. Another example is Medicare and Medicaid—programs with worthy goals but whose costs have increased from 11.2 billion to almost 60 billion, more than 5 times as much, in just 10 years.

Waste and fraud are serious problems. Back in 1980 Federal investigators testified before one of your committees that "corruption has permeated virtually every area of the Medicare and Medicaid health care industry." One official said many of the people who are cheating the system were "very confident that nothing was going to happen to them." Well, something is going to happen. Not only the taxpayers are defrauded; the people with real dependency on these programs are deprived of what they need, because available resources are going not to the needy, but to the greedy.

The time has come to control the uncontrollable. In August we made a start. I signed a bill to reduce the growth of these programs by $44 billion over the next 3 years while at the same time preserving essential services for the truly needy. Shortly you will receive from me a message on further reforms we intend to install—some new, but others long recommended by your own congressional committees. I ask you to help make these savings for the American taxpayer.

The savings we propose in entitlement programs will total some $63 billion over 4 Years and will, without affecting social t security, go a long way toward bringing Federal spending under control.

But don't be fooled by those who proclaim that spending cuts will deprive the elderly, the needy, and the helpless. The. Federal Government will still subsidize 95 million meals every day. That's one out of seven of all the meals served in America. Head Start, senior nutrition programs, and child welfare programs will not be cut from the levels we proposed last year. More than one-half billion dollars has been proposed for minority business assistance. And research at the National Institute of Health will be increased by over $100 million. While meeting all these needs, we intend to plug unwarranted tax loopholes and strengthen the law which requires all large corporations to pay a minimum tax.

I am confident the economic program we've put into operation will protect the needy while it triggers a recovery that will benefit all Americans. It will stimulate the economy, result in increased savings and provide capital for expansion, mortgages for homebuilding, and jobs for the unemployed.

Now that the essentials of that program are in place, our next major undertaking must be a program—just as bold, just as innovative—to make government again accountable to the people, to make our system of federalism work again.

Our citizens feel they've lost control of even the most basic decisions made about the essential services of government, such as schools, welfare, roads, and even garbage collection. And they're right. A maze of interlocking jurisdictions and levels of government confronts average citizens in trying to solve even the simplest of problems. They don't know where to turn for answers, who to hold accountable, who to praise, who to blame, who to vote for or against. The main reason for this is the overpowering growth of Federal grants-in-aid programs during the past few decades.

In 1960 the Federal Government had 132 categorical grant programs, costing $7 billion. When I took office, there were approximately 500, costing nearly a hundred billion dollars--13 programs for energy, 36 for pollution control, 66 for social services, 90 for education. And here in the Congress, it takes at least 166 committees just to try to keep track of them.

You know and I know that neither the President nor the Congress can properly oversee this jungle of grants-in-aid; indeed, the growth of these grants has led to the distortion in the vital functions of government. As one Democratic Governor put it recently: The National Government should be worrying about "arms control, not potholes."

The growth in these Federal programs has—in the words of one intergovernmental commission—made the Federal Government "more pervasive, more intrusive, more unmanageable, more ineffective and costly, and above all, more (un) accountable." Let's solve this problem with a single, bold stroke: the return of some $47 billion in Federal programs to State and local government, together with the means to finance them and a transition period of nearly 10 years to avoid unnecessary disruption.

I will shortly send this Congress a message describing this program. I want to emphasize, however, that its full details will have been worked out only after close consultation with congressional, State, and local officials.

Starting in fiscal 1984, the Federal Government will assume full responsibility for the cost of the rapidly growing Medicaid program to go along with its existing responsibility for Medicare. As part of a financially equal swap, the States will simultaneously take full responsibility for Aid to Families with Dependent Children and food stamps. This will make welfare less costly and more responsive to genuine need, because it'll be designed and administered closer to the grass roots and the people it serves.

In 1984 the Federal Government will apply the full proceeds from certain excise taxes to a grass roots trust fund that will belong in fair shares to the 50 States. The total amount flowing into this fund will be $28 billion a year. Over the next 4 years the States can use this money in either of two ways. If they want to continue receiving Federal grants in such areas as transportation, education, and social services, they can use their trust fund money to pay for the grants. Or to the extent they choose to forgo the Federal grant programs, they can use their trust fund money on their own for those or other purposes. There will be a mandatory pass-through of part of these funds to local governments.

By 1988 the States will be in complete control of over 40 Federal grant programs. The trust fund will start to phase out, eventually to disappear, and the excise taxes will be turned over to the States. They can then preserve, lower, or raise taxes on their own and fund and manage these programs as they see fit.

In a single stroke we will be accomplishing a realignment that will end cumbersome administration and spiraling costs at the Federal level while we ensure these programs will be more responsive to both the people they're meant to help and the people who pay for them.

Hand in hand with this program to strengthen the discretion and flexibility of State and local governments, we're proposing legislation for an experimental effort to improve and develop our depressed urban areas in the 1980's and '90's. This legislation will permit States and localities to apply to the Federal Government for designation as urban enterprise zones. A broad range of special economic incentives in the zones will help attract new business, new jobs, new opportunity to America's inner cities and rural towns. Some will say our mission is to save free enterprise. Well, I say we must free enterprise so that together we can save America.

Some will also say our States and local communities are not up to the challenge of a new and creative partnership. Well, that might have been true 20 years ago before reforms like reapportionment and the Voting Rights Act, the 10-year extension of which I strongly support. It's no longer true today. This administration has faith in State and local governments and the constitutional balance envisioned by the Founding Fathers. We also believe in the integrity, decency, and sound, good sense of grass roots Americans.

Our faith in the American people is reflected in another major endeavor. Our private sector initiatives task force is seeking out successful community models of school, church, business, union, foundation, and civic programs that help community needs. Such groups are almost invariably far more efficient than government in running social programs.

We're not asking them to replace discarded and often discredited government programs dollar for dollar, service for service. We just want to help them perform the good works they choose and help others to profit by their example. Three hundred and eighty-five thousand corporations and private organizations are already working on social programs ranging from drug rehabilitation to job training, and thousands more Americans have written us asking how they can help. The volunteer spirit is still alive and well in America.

Our nation's long journey towards civil rights for all our citizens---once a source of discord, now a source of pride—must continue with no backsliding or slowing down. We must and shall see that those basic laws that guarantee equal rights are preserved and, when necessary, strengthened.

Our concern for equal rights for women is firm and unshakable. We launched a new Task Force on Legal Equity for Women and a Fifty States Project that will examine State laws for discriminatory language. And for the first time in our history, a woman sits on the highest court in the land.

So, too, the problem of crime—one as real and deadly serious as any in America today. It demands that we seek transformation of our legal system, which overly protects the rights of criminals while it leaves society and the innocent victims of crime without justice.

We look forward to the enactment of a responsible clean air act to increase jobs while continuing to improve the quality of our air. We're encouraged by the bipartisan initiative of the House and are hopeful of further progress as the Senate continues its deliberations.

So far, I've concentrated largely, now, on domestic matters. To view the state of the Union in perspective, we must not ignore the rest of the world. There isn't time tonight for a lengthy treatment of social—or foreign policy,

I should say, a subject I intend to address in detail in the near future. A few words, however, are in order on the progress we've made over the past year, reestablishing respect for our nation around the globe and some of the challenges and goals that we will approach in the year ahead.

At Ottawa and Cancun, I met with leaders of the major industrial powers and developing nations. Now, some of those I met with were a little surprised that I didn't apologize for America's wealth. Instead, I spoke of the strength of the free marketplace system and how that system could help them realize their aspirations for economic development and political freedom. I believe lasting friendships were made, and the foundation was laid for future cooperation.

In the vital region of the Caribbean Basin, we're developing a program of aid, trade, and investment incentives to promote self-sustaining growth and a better, more secure life for our neighbors to the south. Toward those who would export terrorism and subversion in the Caribbean and elsewhere, especially Cuba and Libya, we will act with firmness.

Our foreign policy is a policy of strength, fairness, and balance. By restoring America's military credibility, by pursuing peace at the negotiating table wherever both sides are willing to sit down in good faith, and by regaining the respect of America's allies and adversaries alike, we have strengthened our country's position as a force for peace and progress in the world.

When action is called for, we're taking it. Our sanctions against the military dictatorship that has attempted to crush human rights in Poland—and against the Soviet regime behind that military dictatorship-clearly demonstrated to the world that America will not conduct "business as usual" with the forces of oppression. If the events in Poland continue to deteriorate, further measures will follow.

Now, let me also note that private American groups have taken the lead in making January 30th a day of solidarity with the people of Poland. So, too, the European Parliament has called for March 21st to be an international day of support for Afghanistan. Well, I urge all peace-loving peoples to join together on those days, to raise their voices, to speak and pray for freedom.

Meanwhile, we're working for reduction of arms and military activities, as I announced in my address to the Nation last November 18th. We have proposed to the Soviet Union a far-reaching agenda for mutual reduction of military forces and have already initiated negotiations with them in Geneva on intermediate-range nuclear forces. In those talks it is essential that we negotiate from a position of strength. There must be a real incentive for the Soviets to take these talks seriously. This requires that we rebuild our defenses.

In the last decade, while we sought the moderation of Soviet power through a process of restraint and accommodation, the Soviets engaged in an unrelenting buildup of their military forces. The protection of our national security has required that we undertake a substantial program to enhance our military forces.

We have not neglected to strengthen our traditional alliances in Europe and Asia, or to develop key relationships with our partners in the Middle East and other countries. Building a more peaceful world requires a sound strategy and the national resolve to back it up. When radical forces threaten our friends, when economic misfortune creates conditions of instability, when strategically vital parts of the world fall under the shadow of Soviet power, our response can make the difference between peaceful change or disorder and violence. That's why we've laid such stress not only on our own defense but on our vital foreign assistance program. Your recent passage of the Foreign Assistance Act sent a signal to the world that America will not shrink from making the investments necessary for both peace and security. Our foreign policy must be rooted in realism, not naivete or self-delusion.

A recognition of what the Soviet empire is about is the starting point. Winston Churchill, in negotiating with the Soviets, observed that they respect only strength and resolve in their dealings with other nations. That's why we've moved to reconstruct our national defenses. We intend to keep the peace. We will also keep our freedom.

We have made pledges of a new frankness in our public statements and worldwide broadcasts. In the face of a climate of falsehood and misinformation, we've promised the world a season of truth—the truth of our great civilized ideas: individual liberty, representative government, the rule of law under God. We've never needed walls or minefields or barbed wire to keep our people in. Nor do we declare martial law to keep our people from voting for the kind of government they want.

Yes, we have our problems; yes, we're in a time of recession. And it's true, there's no quick fix, as I said, to instantly end the tragic pain of unemployment. But we will end it. The process has already begun, and we'll see its effect as the year goes on.

We speak with pride and admiration of that little band of Americans who overcame insuperable odds to set this nation on course 200 years ago. But our glory didn't end with them. Americans ever since have emulated their deeds.

We don't have to turn to our history books for heroes. They're all around us. One who sits among you here tonight epitomized that heroism at the end of the longest imprisonment ever inflicted on men of our Armed Forces. Who will ever forget that night when we waited for television to bring us the scene of that first plane landing at Clark Field in the Philippines, bringing our POW's home? The plane door opened and Jeremiah Denton came slowly down the ramp. He caught sight of our flag, saluted it, said, "God bless America," and then thanked us for bringing him home.

Just 2 weeks ago, in the midst of a terrible tragedy on the Potomac, we saw again the spirit of American heroism at its finest—the heroism of dedicated rescue workers saving crash victims from icy waters. And we saw the heroism of one of our young government employees,

Lenny Skutnik, who, when he saw a woman lose her grip on the helicopter line, dived into the water and dragged her to safety.

And then there are countless, quiet, everyday heroes of American who sacrifice long and hard so their children will know a better life than they've known; church and civic volunteers who help to feed, clothe, nurse, and teach the needy; millions who've made our nation and our nation's destiny so very special-unsung heroes who may not have realized their own dreams themselves but then who reinvest those dreams in their children. Don't let anyone tell you that America's best days are behind her, that the American spirit has been vanquished. We've seen it triumph too often in our lives to stop believing in it now.

A hundred and twenty years ago, the greatest of all our Presidents delivered his second State of the Union message in this Chamber. "We cannot escape history," Abraham Lincoln warned. "We of this Congress and this administration will be remembered in spite of ourselves." The "trial through which we pass will light us down, in honor or dishonor, to the latest (last) generation."

Well, that President and that Congress did not fail the American people. Together they weathered the storm and preserved the Union. Let it be said of us that we, too, did not fail; that we, too, worked together to bring America through difficult times. Let us so conduct ourselves that two centuries from now, another Congress and another President, meeting in this Chamber as we are meeting, will speak of us with pride, saying that we met the test and preserved for them in their day the sacred flame of liberty—this last, best hope of man on Earth.

God bless you, and thank you. NOTE: The President spoke at 9 p.m. in the House Chamber at the Capitol. He was introduced by Thomas P. O'Neill, Jr., Speaker of the House of Representatives. The address was broadcast live on nationwide radio and television.

THE STATE OF THE UNION

The State of the Union on January 25, 1983

Mr. Speaker, Mr. President, distinguished Members of the Congress, honored guests, and fellow citizens:

This solemn occasion marks the 196th time that a President of the United States has reported on the State of the Union since George Washington first did so in 1790. That's a lot of reports, but there's no shortage of new things to say about the State of the Union. The very key to our success has been our ability, foremost among nations, to preserve our lasting values by making change work for us rather than against us.

I would like to talk with you this evening about what we can do together—not as Republicans and Democrats, but as Americans-to make tomorrow's America happy and prosperous at home, strong and respected abroad, and at peace in the world.

As we gather here tonight, the state of our Union is strong, but our economy is troubled. For too many of our fellow citizens-farmers, steel and auto workers, lumbermen, black teenagers, working mothers-this is a painful period. We must all do everything in our power to bring their ordeal to an end. It has fallen to us, in our time, to undo damage that was a long time in the making, and to begin the hard but necessary task of building a better future for ourselves and our children.

We have a long way to go, but thanks to the courage, patience, and strength of our people, America is on the mend.

But let me give you just one important reason why I believe this—it involves many members of this body.

Just 10 days ago, after months of debate and deadlock, the bipartisan Commission on Social Security accomplished the seemingly impossible. Social security, as some of us had warned for so long, faced disaster. I, myself, have been talking about this problem for almost 30 years. As 1983 began, the system stood on the brink of bankruptcy, a double victim of our economic ills. First, a decade of rampant inflation drained its reserves as we tried to protect beneficiaries from the spiraling cost of living. Then the recession and the sudden end of inflation withered the expanding wage base and increasing revenues the system needs to support the 36 million Americans who depend on it.

When the Speaker of the House, the Senate majority leader, and I performed the bipartisan—or formed the bipartisan Commission on Social Security, pundits and experts predicted that party divisions and conflicting interests would prevent the Commission from agreeing on a plan to save social security. Well, sometimes, even here in Washington, the cynics are wrong. Through compromise and cooperation, the members of the Commission overcame their differences and achieved a fair, workable plan. They proved that, when it comes to the national welfare, Americans can still pull together for the common good.

Tonight, I'm especially pleased to join with the Speaker and the Senate majority leader in urging the Congress to enact this plan by Easter.

There are elements in it, of course, that none of us prefers, but taken together it performs a package that all of us can support. It asks for some sacrifice by all—the self-employed, beneficiaries, workers, government employees, and the better-off among the retired—but it imposes an undue burden on none. And, in supporting it, we keep an important pledge to the American people: The integrity of the social security system will be preserved, and no one's payments will be reduced.

The Commission's plan will do the job; indeed, it must do the job. We owe it to today's older Americans and today's younger workers. So, before we go any further, I ask you to join with me in saluting the members of the Commission who are here tonight and Senate Majority Leader Howard Baker and Speaker Tip O'Neill for a job well done. I hope and pray the bipartisan spirit that guided you in this endeavor will inspire all of us as we face the challenges of the year ahead.

Nearly half a century ago, in this Chamber, another American President, Franklin Delano Roosevelt, in his second State of the Union message, urged America to look to the future, to meet the challenge of change and the need for leadership that looks forward, not backward.

"Throughout the world," he said, "change is the order of the day. In every nation economic problems long in the making have brought crises to (of) many kinds for which the masters of old practice and theory were unprepared." He also reminded us that "the future lies with those wise political leaders who realize that the great public is interested more in Government than in politics."

So, let us, in these next 2 years—men and women of both parties, every political shade—concentrate on the long-range, bipartisan responsibilities of government, not the short-range or short-term temptations of partisan politics.

The problems we inherited were far worse than most inside and out of government had expected; the recession was deeper than most inside and out of government had predicted. Curing those problems has taken more time and a higher toll than any of us wanted. Unemployment is far too high. Projected Federal spending—if government refuses to tighten its own belt-will also be far too high and could weaken and shorten the economic recovery now underway.

This recovery will bring with it a revival of economic confidence and spending for consumer items and capital goods—the stimulus we need to restart our stalled economic engines. The American people have already stepped up their rate of saving, assuring that the funds needed to modernize our factories and improve our technology will once again flow to business and industry.

The inflationary expectations that led to a 21 ½-percent interest prime rate and soaring mortgage rates 2 years ago are now reduced by almost half. Leaders have started to realize that double-digit inflation is no longer a way of life. I misspoke there. I should have said "lenders."

So, interest rates have tumbled, paving the way for recovery in vital industries like housing and autos.

The early evidence of that recovery has started coming in. Housing starts for the fourth quarter of 1982 were up 45 percent from a year ago, and housing permits, a sure indicator of future growth, were up a whopping 60 percent.

We're witnessing an upsurge of productivity and impressive evidence that American industry will once again become competitive in markets at home and abroad, ensuring more jobs and better incomes for the Nation's work force. But our confidence must also be tempered by realism and patience. Quick fixes and artificial stimulants repeatedly applied over decades are what brought us the inflationary disorders that we've now paid such a heavy price to cure.

The permanent recovery in employment, production, and investment we seek won't come in a sharp, short spurt. It'll build carefully and steadily in the months and years ahead. In the meantime, the challenge of government is to identify the things that we can do now to ease the massive economic transition for the American people.

The Federal budget is both a symptom and a cause of our economic problems. Unless we reduce the dangerous growth rate in government spending, we could face the prospect of sluggish economic growth into the indefinite future. Failure to cope with this problem now could mean as much as a trillion dollars more in national debt in the next 4 years alone. That would average $4,300 in additional debt for every man, woman, child, and baby in our nation.

To assure a sustained recovery, we must continue getting runaway spending under control to bring those deficits down. If we don't, the recovery will be too short, unemployment will remain too high, and we will leave an unconscionable burden of national debt for our children. That we must not do.

Let's be clear about where the deficit problem comes from. Contrary to the drumbeat we've been hearing for the last few months, the deficits we face are not rooted in defense spending. Taken as a percentage of the gross national product, our defense spending happens to be only about four-fifths of what it was in 1970. Nor is the deficit, as some would have it, rooted in tax cuts. Even with our tax cuts, taxes as a fraction of gross national product remain about the same as they were in 1970. The fact is, our deficits come from the uncontrolled growth of the budget for domestic spending.

During the 1970's, the share of our national income devoted to this domestic spending increased by more than 60 percent, from 10 cents out of every dollar produced by the American people to 16 cents. In spite of all our economies and efficiencies, and without adding any new programs, basic, necessary domestic spending provided for in this year's budget will grow to almost a trillion dollars over the next 5 years.

The deficit problem is a clear and present danger to the basic health of our Republic. We need a plan to overcome this danger—a plan based on these principles. It must be bipartisan. Conquering the deficits and putting the Government's house in order will require the best effort of all of us. It must be fair. Just as all will share in the benefits that will come from recovery, all would share fairly in the burden of transition. It must be prudent. The strength of our national defense must be restored so that we can pursue prosperity and peace and freedom while maintaining our commitment to the truly needy. And finally, it must be realistic. We can't rely on hope alone.

With these guiding principles in mind, let me outline a four-part plan to increase economic growth and reduce deficits.

First, in my budget message, I will recommend a Federal spending freeze. I know this is strong medicine, but so far, we have only cut the rate of increase in Federal spending. The Government has continued to spend more money each year, though not as much more as it did in the past. Taken as a whole, the budget I'm proposing for the fiscal year will increase no more than the rate of inflation. In other words, the Federal Government will hold the line on real spending. Now, that's far less than many American families have had to do in these difficult times.

I will request that the proposed 6-month freeze in cost-of-living adjustments recommended by the bipartisan Social Security Commission be applied to other government-related retirement programs. I will, also, propose a 1-year freeze on a broad range of domestic spending programs, and for Federal civilian and military pay and pension programs. And let me say right here, I'm sorry, with regard to the military, in asking that of them, because for so many years they have been so far behind and so low in reward for what the men and women in uniform are doing. But I'm sure they will understand that this must be across the board and fair.

Second, I will ask the Congress to adopt specific measures to control the growth of the so-called uncontrollable spending programs. These are the automatic spending programs, such as food stamps, that cannot be simply frozen and that have grown by over 400 percent since 1970. They are the largest single cause of the built-in or structural deficit problem. Our standard here will be fairness, ensuring that the taxpayers' hard-earned dollars go only to the truly needy; that none of them are turned away, but that fraud and waste are stamped out. And I'm sorry to say, there's a lot of it out there. In the food stamp program alone, last year, we identified almost $1.1 billion in overpayments. The taxpayers aren't the only victims of this kind of abuse. The truly needy suffer as funds intended for them are taken not by the needy, but by the greedy. For everyone's sake, we must put an end to such waste and corruption.

Third, I will adjust our program to restore America's defenses by proposing $55 billion in defense savings over the next 5 years. These are savings recommended to me by the Secretary of Defense, who has assured me they can be safely achieved and will not diminish our ability to negotiate arms reductions or endanger America's security. We will not gamble with our national survival.

And fourth, because we must ensure reduction and eventual elimination of deficits over the next several years, I will propose a standby tax, limited to no more than 1 percent of the gross national product, to start in fiscal 1986. It would last no more than 3 years, and it would start only if the Congress has first approved our spending freeze and budget control program. And there are several other conditions also that must be met, all of them in order for this program to be triggered.

Now, you could say that this is an insurance policy for the future, a remedy that will be at hand if needed but only resorted to if absolutely necessary. In the meantime, we'll continue to study ways to simplify the tax code and make it more fair for all Americans. This is a goal that every American who's ever struggled with a tax form can understand.

At the same time, however, I will oppose any efforts to undo the basic tax reforms that we've already enacted, including the 10-percent tax break coming to taxpayers this July and the tax indexing which will protect all Americans from inflationary bracket creep in the years ahead.

Now, I realize that this four-part plan is easier to describe than it will be to enact. But the looming deficits that hang over us and over America's future must be reduced. The path I've outlined is fair, balanced, and realistic. If enacted, it will ensure a steady decline in deficits, aiming toward a balanced budget by the end of the decade. It's the only path that will lead to a strong, sustained recovery. Let us follow that path together.

No domestic challenge is more crucial than providing stable, permanent jobs for all Americans who want to work. The recovery program will provide jobs for most, but others will need special help and training for new skills. Shortly, I will submit to the Congress the Employment Act of 1983, designed to get at the special problems of the long-term unemployed, as well as young people trying to enter the job market. I'll propose extending unemployment benefits, including special incentives to employers who hire the long-term unemployed, providing programs for displaced workers, and helping federally funded and State-administered unemployment insurance programs provide workers with training and relocation assistance. Finally, our proposal will include new incentives for summer youth employment to help young people get a start in the job market.

We must offer both short-term help and long-term hope for our unemployed. I hope we can work together on this. I hope we can work together as we did last year in enacting the landmark Job Training Partnership Act. Regulatory reform legislation, a responsible clean air act, and passage of enterprise zone legislation will also create new incentives for jobs and opportunity.

One of out of every five jobs in our country depends on trade. So, I will propose a broader strategy in the field of international trade—one that increases the openness of our trading system and is fairer to America's farmers and workers in the world marketplace. We must have adequate export financing to sell American products overseas. I will ask for new negotiating authority to remove barriers and to get more of our products into foreign markets. We must strengthen the organization of our trade agencies and make changes in our domestic laws and international trade policy to promote free trade and the increased flow of American goods, services, and investments.

Our trade position can also be improved by making our port system more efficient. Better, more active harbors translate into stable jobs in our coalfields, railroads, trucking industry, and ports. After 2 years of debate, it's time for us to get together and enact a port modernization bill.

Education, training, and retraining are fundamental to our success as are research and development and productivity. Labor, management, and government at all levels can and must participate in improving these tools of growth. Tax policy, regulatory practices, and government programs all need constant reevaluation in terms of our competitiveness. Every American has a role and a stake in international trade.

We Americans are still the technological leaders in most fields. We must keep that edge, and to do so we need to begin renewing the basics—starting with our educational system. While we grew complacent, others have acted. Japan, with a population only about half the size of ours, graduates from its universities more engineers than we do. If a child doesn't receive adequate math and science teaching by the age of 16, he or she has lost the chance to be a scientist or an engineer. We must join together-parents, teachers, grass roots groups, organized labor, and the business community-to revitalize American education by setting a standard of excellence.

In 1983 we seek four major education goals: a quality education initiative to encourage a substantial upgrading of math and science instruction through block grants to the States; establishment of education savings accounts that will give middle and lower-income families an incentive to save for their children's college education and, at the same time, encourage a real increase in savings for economic growth; passage of tuition tax credits for parents who want to send their children to private or religiously affiliated schools; a constitutional amendment to permit voluntary school prayer. God should never have been expelled from America's classrooms in the first place.

Our commitment to fairness means that we must assure legal and economic equity for women, and eliminate, once and for all, all traces of unjust discrimination against women from the United States Code. We will not tolerate wage discrimination based on sex, and we intend to strengthen enforcement of child support laws to ensure that single parents, most of whom are women, do not suffer unfair financial hardship. We will also take action to remedy inequities in pensions. These initiatives will be joined by others to continue our efforts to promote equity for women.

Also in the area of fairness and equity, we will ask for extension of the Civil Rights Commission, which is due to expire this year. The Commission is an important part of the ongoing struggle for justice in America, and we strongly support its reauthorization. Effective enforcement of our nation's fair housing laws is also essential to ensuring equal opportunity. In the year ahead, we'll work to strengthen enforcement of fair housing laws for all Americans.

The time has also come for major reform of our criminal justice statutes and acceleration of the drive against organized crime and drug trafficking. It's high time that we make our cities safe again. This administration hereby declares an all-out war on big-time organized crime and the drug racketeers who are poisoning our young people. We will also implement recommendations of our Task Force on Victims of Crime, which will report to me this week.

American agriculture, the envy of the world, has become the victim of its own successes. With one farmer now producing enough food to feed himself and 77 other people, America is confronted with record surplus crops and commodity prices below the cost of production. We must strive, through innovations like the payment-in-kind crop swap approach and an aggressive export policy, to restore health and vitality to rural America. Meanwhile, I have instructed the Department of Agriculture to work individually with farmers with debt problems to help them through these tough times.

Over the past year, our Task Force on Private Sector Initiatives has successfully forged a working partnership involving leaders of business, labor, education, and government to address the training needs of American workers. Thanks to the Task Force, private sector initiatives are now underway in all 50 States of the Union, and thousands of working people have been helped in making the shift from dead-end jobs and low-demand skills to the growth areas of high technology and the service economy. Additionally, a major effort will be focused on encouraging the expansion of private community child care. The new advisory council on private sector initiatives will carry on and extend this vital work of encouraging private initiative in 1983.

In the coming year, we will also act to improve the quality of life for Americans by curbing the skyrocketing cost of health care that is becoming an unbearable financial burden for so many. And we will submit legislation to provide catastrophic illness insurance coverage for older Americans.

I will also shortly submit a comprehensive federalism proposal that will continue our efforts to restore to States and local governments their roles as dynamic laboratories of change in a creative society.

During the next several weeks, I will send to the Congress a series of detailed proposals on these and other topics and look forward to working with you on the development of these initiatives.

So far, now, I've concentrated mainly on the problems posed by the future. But in almost every home and workplace in America, we're already witnessing reason for great hope—the first flowering of the manmade miracles of high technology, a field pioneered and still led by our country.

To many of us now, computers, silicon chips, data processing, cybernetics, and all the other innovations of the dawning high technology age are as mystifying as the workings of the combustion engine must have been when that first Model T rattled down Main Street, U.S.A. But as surely as America's pioneer spirit made us the industrial giant of the 20th century, the same pioneer spirit today is opening up on another vast front of opportunity, the frontier of high technology.

In conquering the frontier we cannot write off our traditional industries, but we must develop the skills and industries that will make us a pioneer of tomorrow. This administration is committed to keeping America the technological leader of the world now and into the 21st century.

But let us turn briefly to the international arena. America's leadership in the world came to us because of our own strength and because of the values which guide us as a society: free elections, a free press, freedom of religious choice, free trade unions, and above all, freedom for the individual and rejection of the arbitrary power of the state. These values are the bedrock of our strength. They unite us in a stewardship of peace and freedom with our allies and friends in NATO, in Asia, in Latin America, and elsewhere. They are also the values which in the recent past some among us had begun to doubt and view with a cynical eye.

Fortunately, we and our allies have rediscovered the strength of our common democratic values, and we're applying them as a cornerstone of a comprehensive strategy for peace with freedom. In London last year, I announced the commitment of the United States to developing the infrastructure of democracy throughout the world. We intend to pursue this democratic initiative vigorously. The future belongs not to governments and ideologies which oppress their peoples, but to democratic systems of self-government which encourage individual initiative and guarantee personal freedom.

But our strategy for peace with freedom must also be based on strength—economic strength and military strength. A strong American economy is essential to the well-being and security of our friends and allies. The restoration of a strong, healthy American economy has been and remains one of the central pillars of our foreign policy. The progress I've been able to report to you tonight will, I know, be as warmly welcomed by the rest of the world as it is by the American people.

We must also recognize that our own economic well-being is inextricably linked to the world economy. We export over 20 percent of our industrial production, and 40 percent of our farmland produces for export. We will continue to work closely with the industrialized democracies of Europe and Japan and with the International Monetary Fund to ensure it has adequate resources to help bring the world economy back to strong, non-inflationary growth.

As the leader of the West and as a country that has become great and rich because of economic freedom, America must be an unrelenting advocate of free trade. As some nations are tempted to turn to protectionism, our strategy cannot be to follow them, but to lead the way toward freer trade. To this end, in May of this year America will host an economic summit meeting in Williamsburg, Virginia.

As we begin our third year, we have put in place a defense program that redeems the neglect of the past decade. We have developed a realistic military strategy to deter threats to peace and to protect freedom if deterrence fails. Our Armed Forces are finally properly paid; after years of neglect are well trained and becoming better equipped and supplied. And the American uniform is once again worn with pride. Most of the major systems needed for modernizing our defenses are already underway, and we will be addressing one key system, the MX missile, in consultation with the Congress in a few months.

America's foreign policy is once again based on bipartisanship, on realism, strength, full partnership, in consultation with our allies, and constructive negotiation with potential adversaries. From the Middle East to southern Africa to Geneva, American diplomats are taking the initiative to make peace and lower arms levels. We should be proud of our role as peacemakers.

In the Middle East last year, the United States played the major role in ending the tragic fighting in Lebanon and negotiated the withdrawal of the PLO from Beirut.

Last September, I outlined principles to carry on the peace process begun so promisingly at Camp David. All the people of the Middle East should know that in the year ahead we will not flag in our efforts to build on that foundation to bring them the blessings of peace.

In Central America and the Caribbean Basin, we are likewise engaged in a partnership for peace, prosperity, and democracy. Final passage of the remaining portions of our Caribbean Basin Initiative, which passed the House last year, is one of this administration's top legislative priorities for 1983.

The security and economic assistance policies of this administration in Latin America and elsewhere are based on realism and represent a critical investment in the future of the human race. This undertaking is a joint responsibility of the executive and legislative branches, and I'm counting on the cooperation and statesmanship of the Congress to help us meet this essential foreign policy goal.

At the heart of our strategy for peace is our relationship with the Soviet Union. The past year saw a change in Soviet leadership. We're prepared for a positive change in Soviet-American relations. But the Soviet Union must show by deeds as well as words a sincere commitment to respect the rights and sovereignty of the family of nations. Responsible members of the world community do not threaten or invade their neighbors. And they restrain their allies from aggression.

For our part, we're vigorously pursuing arms reduction negotiations with the Soviet Union. Supported by our allies, we've put forward draft agreements proposing significant weapon reductions to equal and verifiable lower levels. We insist on an equal balance of forces. And given the overwhelming evidence of Soviet violations of international treaties concerning chemical and biological weapons, we also insist that any agreement we sign can and will be verifiable.

In the case of intermediate-range nuclear forces, we have proposed the complete elimination of the entire class of land-based missiles. We're also prepared to carefully explore serious Soviet proposals. At the same time, let me emphasize that allied steadfastness remains a key to achieving arms reductions.

With firmness and dedication, we'll continue to negotiate. Deep down, the Soviets must know it's in their interest as well as ours to prevent a wasteful arms race. And once they recognize our unshakable resolve to maintain adequate deterrence, they will have every reason to join us in the search for greater security and major arms reductions. When that moment comes—and I'm confident that it will—we will have taken an important step toward a more peaceful future for all the world's people.

A very wise man, Bernard Baruch, once said that America has never forgotten the nobler things that brought her into being and that light her path. Our country is a special place, because we Americans have always been sustained, through good times and bad, by a noble vision— a vision not only of what the world around us is today but what we as a free people can make it be tomorrow.

We're realists; we solve our problems instead of ignoring them, no matter how loud the chorus of despair around us. But we're also idealists, for it was an ideal that brought our ancestors to these shores from every corner of the world.

Right now we need both realism and idealism. Millions of our neighbors are without work. It is up to us to see they aren't without hope. This is a task for all of us. And may I say, Americans have rallied to this cause, proving once again that we are the most generous people on Earth.

We who are in government must take the lead in restoring the economy. And here all that time, I thought you were reading the paper.

The single thing—the single thing that can start the wheels of industry turning again is further reduction of interest rates. Just another 1 or 2 points can mean tens of thousands of jobs.

Right now, with inflation as low as it is, 3.9 percent, there is room for interest rates to come down. Only fear prevents their reduction. A lender, as we know, must charge an interest rate that recovers the depreciated value of the dollars loaned. And that depreciation is, of course, the amount of inflation. Today, interest rates are based on fear—fear that government will resort to measures, as it has in the past, that will send inflation zooming again.

We who serve here in this Capital must erase that fear by making it absolutely clear that we will not stop fighting inflation; that, together, we will do only those things that will lead to lasting economic growth.

Yes, the problems confronting us are large and forbidding. And, certainly, no one can or should minimize the plight of millions of our friends and neighbors who are living in the bleak emptiness of unemployment. But we must and can give them good reason to be hopeful.

Back over the years, citizens like ourselves have gathered within these walls when our nation was threatened; sometimes when its very existence was at stake. Always with courage and common sense, they met the crises of their time and lived to see a stronger, better, and more prosperous country. The present situation is no worse and, in fact, is not as bad as some of those they faced. Time and again, they proved that there is nothing we Americans cannot achieve as free men and women.

Yes, we still have problems—plenty of them. But it's just plain wrong—unjust to our country and unjust to our people—to let those problems stand in the way of the most important truth of all: America is on the mend.

We owe it to the unfortunate to be aware of their plight and to help them in every way we can. No one can quarrel with that. We must and do have compassion for all the victims of this economic crisis. But the big story about America today is the way that millions of confident, caring people-those extraordinary "ordinary" Americans who never make the headlines and will never be interviewed—are laying the foundation, not just for recovery from our present problems but for a better tomorrow for all our people.

From coast to coast, on the job and in classrooms and laboratories, at new construction sites and in churches and community groups, neighbors are helping neighbors. And they've already begun the building, the research, the work, and the giving that will make our country great again.

I believe this, because I believe in them-in the strength of their hearts and minds, in the commitment that each one of them brings to their daily lives, be they high or humble. The challenge for us in government is to be worthy of them—to make government a help, not a hindrance to our people in the challenging but promising days ahead.

If we do that, if we care what our children and our children's children will say of us, if we want them one day to be thankful for what we did here in these temples of freedom, we will work together to make America better for our having been here-not just in this year or this decade but in the next century and beyond.

Thank you, and God bless you. NOTE: The President spoke at 9:03 p.m. in the House Chamber of the Capitol. He was introduced by Thomas P. O'Neill, Jr., Speaker of the House of Representatives. The address was broadcast live on nationwide radio and television.

The State of the Union on January 25, 1984

Mr. Speaker, Mr. President, distinguished Members of the Congress, honored guests, and fellow citizens:

Once again, in keeping with time-honored tradition, I have come to report to you on the state of the Union, and I'm pleased to report that America is much improved, and there's good reason to believe that improvement will continue through the days to come.

You and I have had some honest and open differences in the year past. But they didn't keep us from joining hands in bipartisan cooperation to stop a long decline that had drained this nation's spirit and eroded its health. There is renewed energy and optimism throughout the land. America is back, standing tall, looking to the eighties with courage, confidence, and hope.

The problems we're overcoming are not the heritage of one person, party, or even one generation. It's just the tendency of government to grow, for practices and programs to become the nearest thing to eternal life we'll ever see on this Earth. And there's always that well-intentioned chorus of voices saying, "With a little more power and a little more money, we could do so much for the people." For a time we forgot the American dream isn't one of making government bigger; it's keeping faith with the mighty spirit of free people under God.

As we came to the decade of the eighties, we faced the worst crisis in our postwar history. In the seventies were years of rising problems and falling confidence. There was a feeling government had grown beyond the consent of the governed. Families felt helpless in the face of mounting inflation and the indignity of taxes that reduced reward for hard work, thrift, and risk taking. All this was overlaid by an ever-growing web of rules and regulations.

On the international scene, we had an uncomfortable feeling that we'd lost the respect of friend and foe. Some questioned whether we had the will to defend peace and freedom. But America is too great for small dreams. There was a hunger in the land for a spiritual revival; if you will, a crusade for renewal. The American people said: Let us look to the future with confidence, both at home and abroad. Let us give freedom a chance.

Americans were ready to make a new beginning, and together we have done it. We're confronting our problems one by one. Hope is alive tonight for millions of young families and senior citizens set free from unfair tax increases and crushing inflation. Inflation has been beaten down from 12.4 to 3.2 percent, and that's a great victory for all the people. The prime rate has been cut almost in half, and we must work together to bring it down even more.

Together, we passed the first across-the-board tax reduction for everyone since the Kennedy tax cuts. Next year, tax rates will be indexed so inflation can't push people into higher brackets when they get cost-of-living pay raises. Government must never again use inflation to profit at the people's expense.

Today a working family earning $25,000 has $1,100 more in purchasing power than if tax and inflation rates were still at the 1980 levels. Real after-tax income increased 5 percent last year. And economic deregulation of key industries like transportation has offered more chances---or choices, I should say, to consumers and new changes---or chances for entrepreneurs and protecting safety. Tonight, we can report and be proud of one of the best recoveries in decades. Send away the handwringers and the doubting Thomases. Hope is reborn for couples dreaming of owning homes and for risk takers with vision to create tomorrow's opportunities.

The spirit of enterprise is sparked by the sunrise industries of high-tech and by small business people with big ideas—people like Barbara Proctor, who rose from a ghetto to build a multimillion-dollar advertising agency in Chicago; Carlos Perez, a Cuban refugee, who turned $27 and a dream into a successful importing business in Coral Gables, Florida.

People like these are heroes for the eighties. They helped 4 million Americans find jobs in 1983. More people are drawing paychecks tonight than ever before. And Congress helps—or progress helps everyone-well, Congress does too----everyone. In 1983 women filled 73 percent of all the new jobs in managerial, professional, and technical fields.

But we know that many of our fellow countrymen are still out of work, wondering what will come of their hopes and dreams. Can we love America and not reach out to tell them: You are not forgotten; we will not rest until each of you can reach as high as your God-given talents will take you.

The heart of America is strong; it's good and true. The cynics were wrong;

America never was a sick society. We're seeing rededication to bedrock values of faith, family, work, neighborhood, peace, and freedom—values that help bring us together as one people, from the youngest child to the most senior citizen.

The Congress deserves America's thanks for helping us restore pride and credibility to our military. And I hope that you're as proud as I am of the young men and women in uniform who have volunteered to man the ramparts in defense of freedom and whose dedication, valor, and skill increases so much our chance of living in a world at peace.

People everywhere hunger for peace and a better life. The tide of the future is a freedom tide, and our struggle for democracy cannot and will not be denied. This nation champions peace that enshrines liberty, democratic rights, and dignity for every individual. America's new strength, confidence, and purpose are carrying hope and opportunity far from our shores. A world economic recovery is underway. It began here.

We've journeyed far, but we have much farther to go. Franklin Roosevelt told us 50 years ago this month:

"Civilization can not go back; civilization must not stand still. We have undertaken new methods. It is our task to perfect, to improve, to alter when necessary, but in all cases to go forward."

It's time to move forward again, time for America to take freedom's next step. Let us unite tonight behind four great goals to keep America free, secure, and at peace in the eighties together.

We can ensure steady economic growth. We can develop America's next frontier. We can strengthen our traditional values. And we can build a meaningful peace to protect our loved ones and this shining star of faith that has guided millions from tyranny to the safe harbor of freedom, progress, and hope.

Doing these things will open wider the gates of opportunity, provide greater security for all, with no barriers of bigotry or discrimination.

The key to a dynamic decade is vigorous economic growth, our first great goal. We might well begin with common sense in Federal budgeting: government spending no more than government takes in.

We must bring Federal deficits down. But how we do that makes all the difference.

We can begin by limiting the size and scope of government. Under the leadership of Vice President Bush, we have reduced the growth of Federal regulations by more than 25 percent and cut well over 300 million hours of government-required paperwork each year. This will save the public more than $150 billion over the next 10 years.

The Grace commission has given us some 2,500 recommendations for reducing wasteful spending, and they're being examined throughout the administration. Federal spending growth has been cut from 17.4 percent in 1980 to less than half of that today, and we have already achieved over $300 billion in budget savings for the period of 1982 to '86. But that's only a little more than half of what we sought. Government is still spending too large a percentage of the total economy.

Now, some insist that any further budget savings must be obtained by reducing the portion spent on defense. This ignores the fact that national defense is solely the responsibility of the Federal Government; indeed, it is its prime responsibility. And yet defense spending is less than a third of the total budget. During the years of President Kennedy and of the years before that, defense was almost half the total budget. And then came several years in which our military capability was allowed to deteriorate to a very dangerous degree. We are just now restoring, through the essential modernization of our conventional and strategic forces, our capability to meet our present and future security needs. We dare not shirk our responsibility to keep America free, secure, and at peace.

The last decade saw domestic spending surge literally out of control. But the basis for such spending had been laid in previous years. A pattern of overspending has been in place for half a century. As the national debt grew, we were told not to worry, that we owed it to ourselves.

Now we know that deficits are a cause for worry. But there's a difference of opinion as to whether taxes should be increased, spending cut, or some of both. Fear is expressed that government borrowing to fund the deficit could inhibit the economic recovery by taking capital needed for business and industrial expansion. Well, I think that debate is missing an important point. Whether government borrows or increases taxes, it will be taking the same amount of money from the private sector, and, either way, that's too much. Simple fairness dictates that government must not raise taxes on families struggling to pay their bills. The root of the problem is that government's share is more than we can afford if we're to have a sound economy.

We must bring down the deficits to ensure continued economic growth. In the budget that I will submit on February 1st, I will recommend measures that will reduce the deficit over the next 5 years. Many of these will be unfinished business from last year's budget.

Some could be enacted quickly if we could join in a serious effort to address this problem. I spoke today with Speaker of the House O'Neill, Senate Majority Leader Baker, Senate Minority Leader Byrd, and House Minority Leader Michel. I asked them if they would designate congressional representatives to meet with representatives of the administration to try to reach prompt agreement on a bipartisan deficit reduction plan. I know it would take a long, hard struggle to agree on a full-scale plan. So, what I have proposed is that we first see if we can agree on a down payment.

Now, I believe there is basis for such an agreement, one that could reduce the deficits by about a hundred billion dollars over the next 3 years. We could focus on some of the less contentious spending cuts that are still pending before the Congress. These could be combined with measures to close certain tax loopholes, measures that the Treasury Department has previously said to be worthy of support. In addition, we could examine the possibility of achieving further outlay savings based on the work of the Grace commission.

If the congressional leadership is willing, my representatives will be prepared to meet with theirs at the earliest possible time. I would hope the leadership might agree on an expedited timetable in which to develop and enact that down payment.

But a down payment alone is not enough to break us out of the deficit problem. It could help us start on the right path. Yet, we must do more. So, I propose that we begin exploring how together we can make structural reforms to curb the built-in growth of spending.

I also propose improvements in the budgeting process. Some 43 of our 50 States grant their Governors the right to veto individual items in appropriation bills without having to veto the entire bill. California is one of those 43 States. As Governor, I found this line-item veto was a powerful tool against wasteful or extravagant spending. It works in 43 States. Let's put it to work in Washington for all the people.

It would be most effective if done by constitutional amendment. The majority of Americans approve of such an amendment, just as they and I approve of an amendment mandating a balanced Federal budget. Many States also have this protection in their constitutions.

To talk of meeting the present situation by increasing taxes is a Band-Aid solution which does nothing to cure an illness that's been coming on for half a century—to say nothing of the fact that it poses a real threat to economic recovery. Let's remember that a substantial amount of income tax is presently owed and not paid by people in the underground economy. It would be immoral to make those who are paying taxes pay more to compensate for those who aren't paying their share.

There's a better way. Let us go forward with an historic reform for fairness, simplicity, and incentives for growth. I am asking Secretary Don Regan for a plan for action to simplify the entire tax code, so all taxpayers, big and small, are treated more fairly. And I believe such a plan could result in that underground economy being brought into the sunlight of honest tax compliance. And it could make the tax base broader, so personal tax rates could come down, not go up. I've asked that specific recommendations, consistent with those objectives, be presented to me by December 1984.

Our second great goal is to build on America's pioneer spirit—I said something funny? I said America's next frontier—and that's to develop that frontier. A sparkling economy spurs initiatives, sunrise industries, and makes older ones more competitive.

Nowhere is this more important than our next frontier: space. Nowhere do we so effectively demonstrate our technological leadership and ability to make life better on Earth. The Space Age is barely a quarter of a century old. But already we've pushed civilization forward with our advances in science and technology. Opportunities and jobs will multiply as we cross new thresholds of knowledge and reach deeper into the unknown.

Our progress in space—taking giant steps for all mankind—is a tribute to American teamwork and excellence. Our finest minds in government, industry, and academia have all pulled together. And we can be proud to say: We are first; we are the best; and we are so because we're free.

America has always been greatest when we dared to be great. We can reach for greatness again. We can follow our dreams to distant stars, living and working in space for peaceful, economic, and scientific gain. Tonight, I am directing NASA to develop a permanently manned space station and to do it within a decade.

A space station will permit quantum leaps in our research in science, communications, in metals, and in lifesaving medicines which could be manufactured only in space. We want our friends to help us meet these challenges and share in their benefits. NASA will invite other countries to participate so we can strengthen peace, build prosperity, and expand freedom for all who share our goals.

Just as the oceans opened up a new world for clipper ships and Yankee traders, space holds enormous potential for commerce today. The market for space transportation could surpass our capacity to develop it. Companies interested in putting payloads into space must have ready access to private sector launch services. The Department of Transportation will help an expendable launch services industry to get off the ground. We'll soon implement a number of executive initiatives, develop proposals to ease regulatory constraints, and, with NASA's help, promote private sector investment in space.

And as we develop the frontier of space, let us remember our responsibility to preserve our older resources here on Earth. Preservation of our environment is not a liberal or conservative challenge, it's common sense.

Though this is a time of budget constraints, I have requested for EPA one of the largest percentage budget increases of any agency. We will begin the long, necessary effort to clean up a productive recreational area and a special national resource—the Chesapeake Bay.

To reduce the threat posed by abandoned hazardous waste dumps, EPA will spend $410 million. And I will request a supplemental increase of 50 million. And because the Superfund law expires in 1985, I've asked Bill Ruckelshaus to develop a proposal for its extension so there'll be additional time to complete this important task.

On the question of acid rain, which concerns people in many areas of the United States and Canada, I'm proposing a research program that doubles our current funding. And we'll take additional action to restore our lakes and develop new technology to reduce pollution that causes acid rain.

We have greatly improved the conditions of our natural resources. We'll ask the Congress for $157 million beginning in 1985 to acquire new park and conservation lands. The Department of the Interior will encourage careful, selective exploration and production on our vital resources in an Exclusive Economic Zone within the 200-mile limit off our coasts—but with strict adherence to environmental laws and with fuller State and public participation.

But our most precious resources, our greatest hope for the future, are the minds and hearts of our people, especially our children. We can help them build tomorrow by strengthening our community of shared values. This must be our third great goal. For us, faith, work, family, neighborhood, freedom, and peace are not just words; they're expressions of what America means, definitions of what makes us a good and loving people.

Families stand at the center of our society. And every family has a personal stake in promoting excellence in education. Excellence does not begin in Washington. A 600-percent increase in Federal spending on education between 1960 and 1980 was accompanied by a steady decline in Scholastic Aptitude Test scores. Excellence must begin in our homes and neighborhood schools, where it's the responsibility of every parent and teacher and the right of every child.

Our children come first, and that's why I established a bipartisan National Commission on Excellence in Education, to help us chart a commonsense course for better education. And already, communities are implementing the Commission's recommendations. Schools are reporting progress in math and reading skills. But we must do more to restore discipline to schools; and we must encourage the teaching of new basics, reward teachers of merit, enforce tougher standards, and put our parents back in charge.

I will continue to press for tuition tax credits to expand opportunities for families and to soften the double payment for those paying public school taxes and private school tuition. Our proposal would target assistance to low- and middle-income families. Just as more incentives are needed within our schools, greater competition is needed among our schools. Without standards and competition, there can be no champions, no records broken, no excellence in education or any other walk of life.

And while I'm on this subject, each day your Members observe a 200-year-old tradition meant to signify America is one nation under God. I must ask: If you can begin your day with a member of the clergy standing right here leading you in prayer, then why can't freedom to acknowledge God be enjoyed again by children in every schoolroom across this land?

America was founded by people who believed that God was their rock of safety. He is ours. I recognize we must be cautious in claiming that God is on our side, but I think it's all right to keep asking if we're on His side.

During our first 3 years, we have joined bipartisan efforts to restore protection of the law to unborn children.

Now, I know this issue is very controversial. But unless and until it can be proven that an unborn child is not a living human being, can we justify assuming without proof that it isn't? No one has yet offered such proof; indeed, all the evidence is to the contrary. We should rise above bitterness and reproach, and if Americans could come together in a spirit of understanding and helping, then we could find positive solutions to the tragedy of abortion.

Economic recovery, better education, rededication to values, all show the spirit of renewal gaining the upper hand. And all will improve family life in the eighties. But families need more. They need assurance that they and their loved ones can walk the streets of America without being afraid. Parents need to know their children will not be victims of child pornography and abduction. This year we will intensify our drive against these and other horrible crimes like sexual abuse and family violence.

Already our efforts to crack down on career criminals, organized crime, drug pushers, and to enforce tougher sentences and paroles are having effect. In 1982 the crime rate dropped by 4.3 percent, the biggest decline since 1972. Protecting victims is just as important as safeguarding the rights of defendants.

Opportunities for all Americans will increase if we move forward in fair housing and work to ensure women's rights, provide for equitable treatment in pension benefits and Individual Retirement Accounts, facilitate child care, and enforce delinquent parent support payments.

It's not just the home but the workplace and community that sustain our values and shape our future. So, I ask your help in assisting more communities to break the bondage of dependency. Help us to free enterprise by permitting debate and voting "yes" on our proposal for enterprise zones in America. This has been before you for 2 years. Its passage can help high-unemployment areas by creating jobs and restoring neighborhoods.

A society bursting with opportunities, reaching for its future with confidence, sustained by faith, fair play, and a conviction that good and courageous people will flourish when they're free—these are the secrets of a strong and prosperous America at peace with itself and the world.

A lasting and meaningful peace is our fourth great goal. It is our highest aspiration. And our record is clear: Americans resort to force only when we must. We have never been aggressors. We have always struggled to defend freedom and democracy.

We have no territorial ambitions. We occupy no countries. We build no walls to lock people in. Americans build the future. And our vision of a better life for farmers, merchants, and working people, from the Americas to Asia, begins with a simple premise: The future is best decided by ballots, not bullets.

Governments which rest upon the consent of the governed do not wage war on their neighbors. Only when people are given a personal stake in deciding their own destiny, benefiting from their own risks, do they create societies that are prosperous, progressive, and free.

Tonight, it is democracies that offer hope by feeding the hungry, prolonging life, and eliminating drudgery.

When it comes to keeping America strong, free, and at peace, there should be no Republicans or Democrats, just patriotic Americans. We can decide the tough issues not by who is right, but by what is right.

Together, we can continue to advance our agenda for peace. We can establish a more stable basis for peaceful relations with the Soviet Union; strengthen allied relations across the board; achieve real and equitable reductions in the levels of nuclear arms; reinforce our peacemaking efforts in the Middle East, Central America, and southern Africa; or assist developing countries, particularly our neighbors in the Western Hemisphere; and assist in the development of democratic institutions throughout the world.

The wisdom of our bipartisan cooperation was seen in the work of the Scowcroft commission, which strengthened our ability to deter war and protect peace. In that same spirit, I urge you to move forward with the Henry Jackson plan to implement the recommendations of the Bipartisan Commission on Central America.

Your joint resolution on the multinational peacekeeping force in Lebanon is also serving the cause of peace. We are making progress in Lebanon. For nearly 10 years, the Lebanese have lived from tragedy to tragedy with no hope for their future. Now the multinational peacekeeping force and our marines are helping them break their cycle of despair. There is hope for a free, independent, and sovereign Lebanon. We must have the courage to give peace a chance. And we must not be driven from our objectives for peace in Lebanon by state-sponsored terrorism. We have seen this ugly specter in Beirut, Kuwait, and Rangoon. It demands international attention. I will forward shortly legislative proposals to help combat terrorism. And I will be seeking support from our allies for concerted action.

Our NATO alliance is strong. 1983 was a banner year for political courage. And we have strengthened our partnerships and our friendships in the Far East. We're committed to dialog, deterrence, and promoting prosperity. We'll work with our trading partners for a new round of negotiations in support of freer world trade, greater competition, and more open markets.

A rebirth of bipartisan cooperation, of economic growth, and military deterrence, and a growing spirit of unity among our people at home and our allies abroad underline a fundamental and far-reaching change: The United States is safer, stronger, and more secure in 1984 than before. We can now move with confidence to seize the opportunities for peace, and we will.

Tonight, I want to speak to the people of the Soviet Union, to tell them it's true that our governments have had serious differences, but our sons and daughters have never fought each other in war. And if we Americans have our way, they never will.

People of the Soviet Union, there is only one sane policy, for your country and mine, to preserve our civilization in this modern age: A nuclear war cannot be won and must never be fought. The only value in our two nations possessing nuclear weapons is to make sure they will never be used. But then would it not be better to do away with them entirely?

People of the Soviet, President Dwight Eisenhower, who fought by your side in World War II, said the essential struggle "is not merely man against man or nation against nation. It is man against war." Americans are people of peace. If your government wants peace, there will be peace. We can come together in faith and friendship to build a safer and far better world for our children and our children's children. And the whole world will rejoice. That is my message to you.

Some days when life seems hard and we reach out for values to sustain us or a friend to help us, we find a person who reminds us what it means to be Americans.

Sergeant Stephen Trujillo, a medic in the 2d Ranger Battalion, 75th Infantry, was in the first helicopter to land at the compound held by Cuban forces in Grenada. He saw three other helicopters crash. Despite the imminent explosion of the burning aircraft, he never hesitated. He ran across 25 yards of open terrain through enemy fire to rescue wounded soldiers. He directed two other medics, administered first aid, and returned again and again to the crash site to carry his wounded friends to safety.

Sergeant Trujillo, you and your fellow service men and women not only saved innocent lives; you set a nation free.

You inspire us as a force for freedom, not for despotism; and, yes, for peace, not conquest. God bless you.

And then there are unsung heroes: single parents, couples, church and civic volunteers. Their hearts carry without complaint the pains of family and community problems. They soothe our sorrow, heal our wounds, calm our fears, and share our joy.

A person like Father Ritter is always there. His Covenant House programs in New York and Houston provide shelter and help to thousands of frightened and abused children each year. The same is true of Dr. Charles Carson. Paralyzed in a plane crash, he still believed nothing is impossible. Today in Minnesota, he works 80 hours a week without pay, helping pioneer the field of computer-controlled walking. He has given hope to 500,000 paralyzed Americans that some day they may walk again.

How can we not believe in the greatness of America? How can we not do what is right and needed to preserve this last best hope of man on Earth? After all our struggles to restore America, to revive confidence in our country, hope for our future, after all our hard-won victories earned through the patience and courage of every citizen, we cannot, must not, and will not turn back. We will finish our job. How could we do less? We're Americans.

Carl Sandburg said, "I see America not in the setting sun of a black night of despair · . . I see America in the crimson light of a rising sun fresh from the burning, creative hand of God... I see great days ahead for men and women of will and vision."

I've never felt more strongly that America's best days and democracy's best days lie ahead. We're a powerful force for good. With faith and courage, we can perform great deeds and take freedom's next step. And we will. We will carry on the tradition of a good and worthy people who have brought light where there was darkness, warmth where there was cold, medicine where there was disease, food where there was hunger, and peace where there was only bloodshed.

Let us be sure that those who come after will say of us in our time, that in our time we did everything that could be done. We finished the race; we kept them free; we kept the faith.

Thank you very much. God bless you, and God bless America. NOTE: The President spoke at 9:02 p.m. in the House Chamber of the Capitol He was introduced by Thomas P. O'Neill, Jr., Speaker of the House of Representatives. The address was broadcast live on nationwide radio and television.

Second Inaugural Address of Ronald Reagan

MONDAY, JANUARY 21, 1985

Senator Mathias, Chief Justice Burger, Vice President Bush, Speaker O'Neill, Senator Dole, Reverend Clergy, members of my family and friends, and my fellow citizens:

This day has been made brighter with the presence here of one who, for a time, has been absent—Senator John Stennis.

God bless you and welcome back.

There is, however, one who is not with us today: Representative Gillis Long of Louisiana left us last night. I wonder if we could all join in a moment of silent prayer. (Moment of silent prayer.) Amen.

There are no words adequate to express my thanks for the great honor that you have bestowed on me. I will do my utmost to be deserving of your trust.

This is, as Senator Mathias told us, the 50th time that we the people have celebrated this historic occasion. When the first President, George Washington, placed his hand upon the Bible, he stood less than a single day's journey by horseback from raw, untamed wilderness. There were 4 million Americans in a union of 13 States. Today we are 60 times as many in a union of 50 States. We have lighted the world with our inventions, gone to the aid of mankind wherever in the world there was a cry for help, journeyed to the Moon and safely returned. So much has changed. And yet we stand together as we did two centuries ago.

When I took this oath four years ago, I did so in a time of economic stress. Voices were raised saying we had to look to our past for the greatness and glory. But we, the present-day Americans, are not given to looking backward. In this blessed land, there is always a better tomorrow.

Four years ago, I spoke to you of a new beginning and we have accomplished that. But in another sense, our new beginning is a continuation of that beginning created two centuries ago when, for the first time in history, government, the people said, was not our master, it is our servant; its only power that which we the people allow it to have.

That system has never failed us, but, for a time, we failed the system. We asked things of government that government was not equipped to give. We yielded authority to the National Government that properly belonged to States or to local governments or to the people themselves. We allowed taxes and inflation to rob us of our earnings and savings and watched the great industrial machine that had made us the most productive people on Earth slow down and the number of unemployed increase.

By 1980, we knew it was time to renew our faith, to strive with all our strength toward the ultimate in individual freedom consistent with an orderly society.

We believed then and now there are no limits to growth and human progress when men and women are free to follow their dreams.

And we were right to believe that. Tax rates have been reduced, inflation cut dramatically, and more people are employed than ever before in our history.

We are creating a nation once again vibrant, robust, and alive. But there are many mountains yet to climb. We will not rest until every American enjoys the fullness of freedom, dignity, and opportunity as our birthright. It is our birthright as citizens of this great Republic, and we'll meet this challenge.

These will be years when Americans have restored their confidence and tradition of progress; when our values of faith, family, work, and neighborhood were restated for a modern age; when our economy was finally freed from government's grip; when we made sincere efforts at meaningful arms reduction, rebuilding our defenses, our economy, and developing new technologies, and helped preserve peace in a troubled world; when Americans courageously supported the struggle for liberty, self-government, and free enterprise throughout the world, and turned the tide of history away from totalitarian darkness and into the warm sunlight of human freedom.

My fellow citizens, our Nation is poised for greatness. We must do what we know is right and do it with all our might. Let history say of us, "These were golden years— when the American Revolution was reborn, when freedom gained new life, when America reached for her best."

Our two-party system has served us well over the years, but never better than in those times of great challenge when we came together not as Democrats or Republicans, but as Americans united in a common cause.

Two of our Founding Fathers, a Boston lawyer named Adams and a Virginia planter named Jefferson, members of that remarkable group who met in Independence Hall and dared to think they could start the world over again, left us an important lesson. They had become political rivals in the Presidential election of 1800. Then years later, when both were retired, and age had softened their anger, they began to speak to each other again through letters. A bond was reestablished between those two who had helped create this government of ours.

In 1826, the 50th anniversary of the Declaration of Independence, they both died. They died on the same day, within a few hours of each other, and that day was the Fourth of July.

In one of those letters exchanged in the sunset of their lives, Jefferson wrote: "It carries me back to the times when, beset with difficulties and dangers, we were fellow laborers in the same cause, struggling for what is most valuable to man, his right to self-government. Laboring always at the same oar, with some wave ever ahead threatening to overwhelm us, and yet passing harmless ... we rode through the storm with heart and hand."

Well, with heart and hand, let us stand as one today: One people under God determined that our future shall be worthy of our past. As we do, we must not repeat the well-intentioned errors of our past. We must never again abuse the trust of working men and women, by sending their earnings on a futile chase after the spiraling demands of a bloated Federal Establishment. You elected us in 1980 to end this prescription for disaster, and I don't believe you reelected us in 1984 to reverse course.

At the heart of our efforts is one idea vindicated by 25 straight months of economic growth: Freedom and incentives unleash the drive and entrepreneurial genius that are the core of human progress. We have begun to increase the rewards for work, savings, and investment; reduce the increase in the cost and size of government and its interference in people's lives.

We must simplify our tax system, make it more fair, and bring the rates down for all who work and earn. We must think anew and move with a new boldness, so every American who seeks work can find work; so the least among us shall have an equal chance to achieve the greatest things—to be heroes who heal our sick, feed the hungry, protect peace among nations, and leave this world a better place.

The time has come for a new American emancipation—a great national drive to tear down economic barriers and liberate the spirit of enterprise in the most distressed areas of our country. My friends, together we can do this, and do it we must, so help me God.—From new freedom will spring new opportunities for growth, a more productive, fulfilled and united people, and a stronger America—an America that will lead the technological revolution, and also open its mind and heart and soul to the treasures of literature, music, and poetry, and the values of faith, courage, and love.

A dynamic economy, with more citizens working and paying taxes, will be our strongest tool to bring down budget deficits. But an almost unbroken 50 years of deficit spending has finally brought us to a time of reckoning. We have come to a turning point, a moment for hard decisions. I have asked the Cabinet and my staff a question, and now I put the same question to all of you: If not us, who? And if not now, when? It must be done by all of us going forward with a program aimed at reaching a balanced budget. We can then begin reducing the national debt.

I will shortly submit a budget to the Congress aimed at freezing government program spending for the next year. Beyond that, we must take further steps to permanently control Government's power to tax and spend. We must act now to protect future generations from Government's desire to spend its citizens' money and tax them into servitude when the bills come due. Let us make it unconstitutional for the Federal Government to spend more than the Federal Government takes in.

We have already started returning to the people and to State and local governments responsibilities better handled by them. Now, there is a place for the Federal Government in matters of social compassion. But our fundamental goals must be to reduce dependency and upgrade the dignity of those who are infirm or disadvantaged. And here a growing economy and support from family and community offer our best chance for a society where compassion is a way of life, where the old and infirm are cared for, the young and, yes, the unborn protected, and the unfortunate looked after and made self.

And there is another area where the Federal Government can play a part. As an older American, I remember a time when people of different race, creed, or ethnic origin in our land found hatred and prejudice installed in social custom and, yes, in law. There is no story more heartening in our history than the progress that we have made toward the "brotherhood of man" that God intended for us. Let us resolve there will be no turning back or hesitation on the road to an America rich in dignity and abundant with opportunity for all our citizens.

Let us resolve that we the people will build an American opportunity society in which all of us—white and black, rich and poor, young and old—will go forward together arm in arm. Again, let us remember that though our heritage is one of blood lines from every corner of the Earth, we are all Americans pledged to carry on this last, best hope of man on Earth.

I have spoken of our domestic goals and the limitations which we should put on our National Government. Now let me turn to a task which is the primary responsibility of National Government-the safety and security of our people.

Today, we utter no prayer more fervently than the ancient prayer for peace on Earth. Yet history has shown that peace will not come, nor will our freedom be preserved, by good will alone. There are those in the world who scorn our vision of human dignity and freedom. One nation, the Soviet Union, has conducted the greatest military buildup in the history of man, building arsenals of awesome offensive weapons.

We have made progress in restoring our defense capability. But much remains to be done. There must be no wavering by us, nor any doubts by others, that America will meet her responsibilities to remain free, secure, and at peace.

There is only one way safely and legitimately to reduce the cost of national security, and that is to reduce the need for it. And this we are trying to do in negotiations with the Soviet Union. We are not just discussing limits on a further increase of nuclear weapons. We seek, instead, to reduce their number. We seek the total elimination one day of nuclear weapons from the face of the Earth.

Now, for decades, we and the Soviets have lived under the threat of mutual assured destruction; if either resorted to the use of nuclear weapons, the other could retaliate and destroy the one who had started it. Is there either logic or morality in believing that if one side threatens to kill tens of millions of our people, our only recourse is to threaten killing tens of millions of theirs?

I have approved a research program to find, if we can, a security shield that would destroy nuclear missiles before they reach their target. It wouldn't kill people, it would destroy weapons. It wouldn't militarize space, it would help demilitarize the arsenals of Earth. It would render nuclear weapons obsolete. We will meet with the Soviets, hoping that we can agree on a way to rid the world of the threat of nuclear destruction.

We strive for peace and security, heartened by the changes all around us. Since the turn of the century, the number of democracies in the world has grown fourfold. Human freedom is on the march, and nowhere more so than our own hemisphere. Freedom is one of the deepest and noblest aspirations of the human spirit. People, worldwide, hunger for the right of self-determination, for those inalienable rights that make for human dignity and progress.

America must remain freedom's staunchest friend, for freedom is our best ally.

And it is the world's only hope, to conquer poverty and preserve peace. Every blow we inflict against poverty will be a blow against its dark allies of oppression and war. Every victory for human freedom will be a victory for world peace.

So we go forward today, a nation still mighty in its youth and powerful in its purpose. With our alliances strengthened, with our economy leading the world to a new age of economic expansion, we look forward to a world rich in possibilities. And all this because we have worked and acted together, not as members of political parties, but as Americans.

My friends, we live in a world that is lit by lightning. So much is changing and will change, but so much endures, and transcends time.

History is a ribbon, always unfurling; history is a journey. And as we continue our journey, we think of those who traveled before us. We stand together again at the steps of this symbol of our democracy—or we would have been standing at the steps if it hadn't gotten so cold. Now we are standing inside this symbol of our democracy. Now we hear again the echoes of our past: a general falls to his knees in the hard snow of Valley Forge; a lonely President paces the darkened halls, and ponders his struggle to preserve the Union; the men of the Alamo call out encouragement to each other; a settler pushes west and sings a song, and the song echoes out forever and fills the unknowing air.

It is the American sound. It is hopeful, big-hearted, idealistic, daring, decent, and fair. That's our heritage; that is our song. We sing it still. For all our problems, our differences, we are together as of old, as we raise our voices to the God who is the Author of this most tender music. And may He continue to hold us close as we fill the world with our sound—sound in unity, affection, and love—one people under God, dedicated to the dream of freedom that He has placed in the human heart, called upon now to pass that dream on to a waiting and hopeful world.

God bless you and may God bless America.

The State of the Union on February 6, 1985

Mr. Speaker, Mr. President, distinguished Members of the Congress, honored guests, and fellow citizens:

I come before you to report on the state of our Union, and I'm pleased to report that after 4 years of united effort, the American people have brought forth a nation renewed, stronger, freer, and more secure than before.

Four years ago we began to change, forever I hope, our assumptions about government and its place in our lives. Out of that change has come great and robust growth-in our confidence, our economy, and our role in the world.

Tonight America is stronger because of the values that we hold dear. We believe faith and freedom must be our guiding stars, for they show us truth, they make us brave, give us hope, and leave us wiser than we were. Our progress began not in Washington, DC, but in the hearts of our families, communities, workplaces, and voluntary groups which, together, are unleashing the invincible spirit of one great nation under God.

Four years ago we said we would invigorate our economy by giving people greater freedom and incentives to take risks and letting them keep more of what they earned. We did what we promised, and a great industrial giant is reborn.

Tonight we can take pride in 25 straight months of economic growth, the strongest in 34 years; a 3-year inflation average of 3.9 percent, the lowest in 17 years; and 7.3 million new jobs in 2 years, with more of our citizens working than ever before.

New freedom in our lives has planted the rich seeds for future success:

For an America of wisdom that honors the family, knowing that if (as) the family goes, so goes our civilization;

For an America of vision that sees tomorrow's dreams in the learning and hard work we do today;

For an America of courage whose service men and women, even as we meet, proudly stand watch on the frontiers of freedom;

For an America of compassion that opens its heart to those who cry out for help.

We have begun well. But it's only a beginning. We're not here to congratulate ourselves on what we have done but to challenge ourselves to finish what has not yet been done.

We're here to speak for millions in our inner cities who long for real jobs, safe neighborhoods, and schools that truly teach. We're here to speak for the American farmer, the entrepreneur, and every worker in industries fighting to modernize and compete. And, yes, we're here to stand, and proudly so, for all who struggle to break free from totalitarianism, for all who know in their hearts that freedom is the one true path to peace and human happiness.

Proverbs tell us, without a vision the people perish. When asked what great principle holds our Union together, Abraham Lincoln said: "Something in (the) Declaration giving liberty, not alone to the people of this country, but hope to the world for all future time."

We honor the giants of our history not by going back but forward to the dreams their vision foresaw. My fellow citizens, this nation is poised for greatness. The time has come to proceed toward a great new challenge—a second American Revolution of hope and opportunity; a revolution carrying us to new heights of progress by pushing back frontiers of knowledge and space; a revolution of spirit that taps the soul of America, enabling us to summon greater strength than we've ever known; and a revolution that carries beyond our shores the golden promise of human freedom in a world of peace.

Let us begin by challenging our conventional wisdom. There are no constraints on the human mind, no walls around the human spirit, no barriers to our progress except those we ourselves erect. Already, pushing down tax rates has freed our economy to vault forward to record growth.

In Europe, they're calling it "the American Miracle." Day by day, we're shattering accepted notions of what is possible. When I was growing up, we failed to see how a new thing called radio would transform our marketplace. Well, today, many have not yet seen how advances in technology are transforming our lives.

In the late 1950's workers at the AT&T semiconductor plant in Pennsylvania produced five transistors a day for $7.50 apiece. They now produce over a million for less than a penny apiece.

New laser techniques could revolutionize heart bypass surgery, cut diagnosis time for viruses linked to cancer from weeks to minutes, reduce hospital costs dramatically, and hold out new promise for saving human lives.

Our automobile industry has overhauled assembly lines, increased worker productivity, and is competitive once again.

We stand on the threshold of a great ability to produce more, do more, be more. Our economy is not getting older and weaker; it's getting younger and stronger. It doesn't need rest and supervision; it needs new challenge, greater freedom. And that word "freedom" is the key to the second American revolution that we need to bring about.

Let us move together with an historic reform of tax simplification for fairness and growth. Last year I asked Treasury Secretary-then-Regan to develop a plan to simplify the tax code, so all taxpayers would be treated more fairly and personal tax rates could come further down.

We have cut tax rates by almost 25 percent, yet the tax system remains unfair and limits our potential for growth. Exclusions and exemptions cause similar incomes to be taxed at different levels. Low-income families face steep tax barriers that make hard lives even harder. The Treasury Department has produced an excellent reform plan, whose principles will guide the final proposal that we will ask you to enact.

One thing that tax reform will not be is a tax increase in disguise. We will not jeopardize the mortgage interest deduction that families need. We will reduce personal tax rates as low as possible by removing many tax preferences. We will propose a top rate of no more than 35 percent, and possibly lower. And we will propose reducing corporate rates, while maintaining incentives for capital formation.

To encourage opportunity and jobs rather than dependency and welfare, we will propose that individuals living at or near the poverty line be totally exempt from Federal income tax. To restore fairness to families, we will propose increasing significantly the personal exemption.

And tonight, I am instructing Treasury Secretary James Baker—I have to get used to saying that—to begin working with congressional authors and committees for bipartisan legislation conforming to these principles. We will call upon the American people for support and upon every man and woman in this Chamber. Together, we can pass, this year, a tax bill for fairness, simplicity, and growth, making this economy the engine of our dreams and America the investment capital of the world. So let us begin.

Tax simplification will be a giant step toward unleashing the tremendous pent-up power of our economy. But a second American revolution must carry the promise of opportunity for all. It is time to liberate the spirit of enterprise in the most distressed areas of our country.

This government will meet its responsibility to help those in need. But policies that increase dependency, break up families, and destroy self-respect are not progressive; they're reactionary. Despite our strides in civil rights, blacks, Hispanics, and all minorities will not have full and equal power until they have full economic power.

We have repeatedly sought passage of enterprise zones to help those in the abandoned corners of our land find jobs, learn skills, and build better lives. This legislation is supported by a majority of you.

Mr. Speaker, I know we agree that 'there must be no forgotten Americans. Let us place new dreams in a million hearts and create a new generation of entrepreneurs by passing enterprise zones this year. And, Tip, you could make that a birthday present.

Nor must we lose the chance to pass our youth employment opportunity wage proposal. We can help teenagers, who have the highest unemployment rate, find summer jobs, so they can know the pride of work and have confidence in their futures.

We'll continue to support the Job Training Partnership Act, which has a nearly two-thirds job placement rate. Credits in education and health care vouchers will help working families shop for services that they need.

Our administration is already encouraging certain low-income public housing residents to own and manage their own dwellings. It's time that all public housing residents have that opportunity of ownership.

The Federal Government can help create a new atmosphere of freedom. But States and localities, many of which enjoy surpluses from the recovery, must not permit their tax and regulatory policies to stand as barriers to growth.

Let us resolve that we will stop spreading dependency and start spreading opportunity; that we will stop spreading bondage and start spreading freedom.

There are some who say that growth initiatives must await final action on deficit reductions. Well, the best way to reduce deficits is through economic growth. More businesses will be started, more investments made, more jobs created, and more people will be on payrolls paying taxes. The best way to reduce government spending is to reduce the need for spending by increasing prosperity. Each added percentage point per year of real GNP growth will lead to cumulative reduction in deficits of nearly $200 billion over 5 years.

To move steadily toward a balanced budget, we must also lighten government's claim on our total economy. We will not do this by raising taxes. We must make sure that our economy grows faster than the growth in spending by the Federal Government. In our fiscal year 1986 budget, overall government program spending will be frozen at the current level. It must not be one dime higher than fiscal year 1985, and three points are key.

First, the social safety net for the elderly, the needy, the disabled, and unemployed will be left intact. Growth of our major health care programs, Medicare and Medicaid, will be slowed, but protections for the elderly and needy will be preserved.

Second, we must not relax our efforts to restore military strength just as we near our goal of a fully equipped, trained, and ready professional corps. National security is government's first responsibility; so in past years defense spending took about half the Federal budget. Today it takes less than a third. We've already reduced our planned defense expenditures by nearly a hundred billion dollars over the past 4 years and reduced projected spending again this year.

You know, we only have a military-industrial complex until a time of danger, and then it becomes the arsenal of democracy. Spending for defense is investing in things that are priceless—peace and freedom.

Third, we must reduce or eliminate costly government subsidies. For example, deregulation of the airline industry has led to cheaper airfares, but on Amtrak taxpayers pay about $35 per passenger every time an Amtrak train leaves the station, It's time we ended this huge Federal subsidy.

Our farm program costs have quadrupled in recent years. Yet I know from visiting farmers, many in great financial distress, that we need an orderly transition to a market-oriented farm economy. We can help farmers best not by expanding Federal payments but by making fundamental reforms, keeping interest rates heading down, and knocking down foreign trade barriers to American farm exports.

We're moving ahead with Grace commission reforms to eliminate waste and improve government's management practices. In the long run, we must protect the taxpayers from government. And I ask again that you pass, as 32 States have now called for, an amendment mandating the Federal Government spend no more than it takes in. And I ask for the authority, used responsibly by 43 Governors, to veto individual items in appropriation bills. Senator Mattingly has introduced a bill permitting a 2-year trial run of the line-item veto. I hope you'll pass and send that legislation to my desk.

Nearly 50 years of government living beyond its means has brought us to a time of reckoning. Ours is but a moment in history. But one moment of courage, idealism, and bipartisan unity can change American history forever.

Sound monetary policy is key to long-running economic strength and stability. We will continue to cooperate with the Federal Reserve Board, seeking a steady policy that ensures price stability without keeping interest rates artificially high or needlessly holding down growth.

Reducing unneeded red tape and regulations, and deregulating the energy, transportation, and financial industries have unleashed new competition, giving consumers more choices, better services, and lower prices. In just one set of grant programs we have reduced 905 pages of regulations to 31. We seek to fully deregulate natural gas to bring on new supplies and bring us closer to energy independence. Consistent with safety standards, we will continue removing restraints on the bus and railroad industries, we will soon end up legislation---or send up legislation, I should say—to return Conrail to the private sector where it belongs, and we will support further deregulation of the trucking industry.

Every dollar the Federal Government does not take from us, every decision it does not make for us will make our economy stronger, our lives more abundant, our future more free.

Our second American revolution will push on to new possibilities not only on Earth but in the next frontier of space. Despite budget restraints, we will seek record funding for research and development.

We've seen the success of the space shuttle. Now we're going to develop a permanently manned space station and new opportunities for free enterprise, because in the next decade Americans and our friends around the world will be living and working together in space.

In the zero gravity of space, we could manufacture in 30 days lifesaving medicines it would take 30 years to make on Earth. We can make crystals of exceptional purity to produce super computers, creating jobs, technologies, and medical breakthroughs beyond anything we ever dreamed possible.

As we do all this, we'll continue to protect our natural resources. We will seek reauthorization and expanded funding for the Superfund program to continue cleaning up hazardous waste sites which threaten human health and the environment.

Now, there's another great heritage to speak of this evening. Of all the changes that have swept America the past 4 years, none brings greater promise than our rediscovery of the values of faith, freedom, family, work, and neighborhood.

We see signs of renewal in increased attendance in places of worship; renewed optimism and faith in our future; love of country rediscovered by our young, who are leading the way. We've rediscovered that work is good in and of itself, that it ennobles us to create and contribute no matter how seemingly humble our jobs. We've seen a powerful new current from an old and honorable tradition—American generosity.

From thousands answering Peace Corps appeals to help boost food production in Africa, to millions volunteering time, corporations adopting schools, and communities pulling together to help the neediest among us at home, we have re-found our values. Private sector initiatives are crucial to our future.

I thank the Congress for passing equal access legislation giving religious groups the same right to use classrooms after school that other groups enjoy. But no citizen need tremble, nor the world shudder, if a child stands in a classroom and breathes a prayer. We ask you again, give children back a right they had for a century and a half or more in this country.

The question of abortion grips our nation. Abortion is either the taking of a human life or it isn't. And if it is—and medical technology is increasingly showing it is—it must be stopped. It is a terrible irony that while some turn to abortion, so many others who cannot become parents cry out for children to adopt. We have room for these children. We can fill the cradles of those who want a child to love. And tonight I ask you in the Congress to move this year on legislation to protect the unborn.

In the area of education, we're returning to excellence, and again, the heroes are our people, not government. We're stressing basics of discipline, rigorous testing, and homework, while helping children become computer-smart as well. For 20 years scholastic aptitude test scores of our high school students went down, but now they have gone up 2 of the last 3 years. We must go forward in our commitment to the new basics, giving parents greater authority and making sure good teachers are rewarded for hard work and achievement through merit pay.

Of all the changes in the past 20 years, none has more threatened our sense of national well-being than the explosion of violent crime. One does not have to be attacked to be a victim. The woman who must run to her car after shopping at night is a victim. The couple draping their door with locks and chains are victims; as is the tired, decent cleaning woman who can't ride a subway home without being afraid.

We do not seek to violate the rights of defendants. But shouldn't we feel more compassion for the victims of crime than for those who commit crime? For the first time in 20 years, the crime index has fallen 2 years in a row. We've convicted over 7,400 drug offenders and put them, as well as leaders of organized crime, behind bars in record numbers.

But we must do more. I urge the House to follow the Senate and enact proposals permitting use of all reliable evidence that police officers acquire in good faith. These proposals would also reform the habeas corpus laws and allow, in keeping with the will of the overwhelming majority of Americans, the use of the death penalty where necessary.

There can be no economic revival in ghettos when the most violent among us are allowed to roam free. It's time we restored domestic tranquility. And we mean to do just that.

Just as we're positioned as never before to secure justice in our economy, we're poised as never before to create a safer, freer, more peaceful world. Our alliances are stronger than ever. Our economy is stronger than ever. We have resumed our historic role as a leader of the free world. And all of these together are a great force for peace.

Since 1981 we've been committed to seeking fair and verifiable arms agreements that would lower the risk of war and reduce the size of nuclear arsenals. Now our determination to maintain a strong defense has influenced the Soviet Union to return to the bargaining table. Our negotiators must be able to go to that table with the united support of the American people. All of us have no greater dream than to see the day when nuclear weapons are banned from this Earth forever.

Each Member of the Congress has a role to play in modernizing our defenses, thus supporting our chances for a meaningful arms agreement. Your vote this spring on the

Peacekeeper missile will be a critical test of our resolve to maintain the strength we need and move toward mutual and verifiable arms reductions.

For the past 20 years we've believed that no war will be launched as long as each side knows it can retaliate with a deadly counterstrike. Well, I believe there's a better way of eliminating the threat of nuclear war. It is a Strategic Defense Initiative aimed ultimately at finding a nonnuclear defense against ballistic missiles. It's the most hopeful possibility of the nuclear age. But it's not very well understood.

Some say it will bring war to the heavens, but its purpose is to deter war in the heavens and on Earth. Now, some say the research would be expensive. Perhaps, but it could save millions of lives, indeed humanity itself. And some say if we build such a system, the Soviets will build a defense system of their own. Well, they already have strategic defenses that surpass ours; a civil defense system, where we have almost none; and a research program covering roughly the same areas of technology that we're now exploring. And finally some say the research will take a long time. Well, the answer to that is: Let's get started.

Harry Truman once said that, ultimately, our security and the world's hopes for peace and human progress "lie not in measures of defense or in the control of weapons, but in the growth and expansion of freedom and self-government."

And tonight, we declare anew to our fellow citizens of the world: Freedom is not the sole prerogative of a chosen few; it is the universal right of all God's children. Look to where peace and prosperity flourish today. It is in homes that freedom built. Victories against poverty are greatest and peace most secure where people live by laws that ensure free press, free speech, and freedom to worship, vote, and create wealth.

Our mission is to nourish and defend freedom and democracy, and to communicate these ideals everywhere we can. America's economic success is freedom's success; it can be repeated a hundred times in a hundred different nations. Many countries in east Asia and the Pacific have few resources other than the enterprise of their own people. But through low tax rates and free markets they've soared ahead of centralized economies. And now China is opening up its economy to meet its needs.

We need a stronger and simpler approach to the process of making and implementing trade policy, and we'll be studying potential changes in that process in the next few weeks. We've seen the benefits of free trade and lived through the disasters of protectionism. Tonight I ask all our trading partners, developed and developing alike, to join us in a new round of trade negotiations to expand trade and competition and strengthen the global economy—and to begin it in this next year.

There are more than 3 billion human beings living in Third World countries with an average per capita income of $650 a year. Many are victims of dictatorships that impoverished them with taxation and corruption. Let us ask our allies to join us in a practical program of trade and assistance that fosters economic development through personal incentives to help these people climb from poverty on their own.

We cannot play innocents abroad in a world that's not innocent; nor can we be passive when freedom is under siege. Without resources, diplomacy cannot succeed. Our security assistance programs help friendly governments defend themselves and give them confidence to work for peace. And I hope that you in the Congress will understand that, dollar for dollar, security assistance contributes as much to global security as our own defense budget.

We must stand by all our democratic allies. And we must not break faith with those who are risking their lives---on every continent, from Afghanistan to Nicaragua—to defy Soviet-supported aggression and secure rights which have been ours from birth.

The Sandinista dictatorship of Nicaragua, with full Cuban-Soviet bloc support, not only persecutes its people, the church, and denies a free press, but arms and provides bases for Communist terrorists attacking neighboring states. Support for freedom fighters is self-defense and totally consistent with the OAS and U.N. Charters. It is essential that the Congress continue all facets of our assistance to Central America. I want to work with you to support the democratic forces whose struggle is tied to our own security.

And tonight, I've spoken of great plans and great dreams. They're dreams we can make come true. Two hundred years of American history should have taught us that nothing is impossible.

Ten years ago a young girl left Vietnam with her family, part of the exodus that followed the fall of Saigon. They came to the United States with no possessions and not knowing a word of English. Ten years ago—the young girl studied hard, learned English, and finished high school in the top of her class. And this May, May 22d to be exact, is a big date on her calendar. Just 10 years from the time she left Vietnam, she will graduate from the United States Military Academy at West Point. I thought you might like to meet an American hero named Jean Nguyen.

Now, there's someone else here tonight, born 79 years ago. She lives in the inner city, where she cares for infants born of mothers who are heroin addicts. The children, born in withdrawal, are sometimes even dropped on her doorstep. She helps them with love. Go to her house some night, and maybe you'll see her silhouette against the window as she walks the floor talking softly, soothing a child in her arms-Mother Hale of Harlem, and she, too, is an American hero.

Jean, Mother Hale, your lives tell us that the oldest American saying is new again: Anything is possible in America if we have the faith, the will, and the heart. History is asking us once again to be a force for good in the world. Let us begin in unity, with justice, and love.

Thank you, and God bless you. NOTE: The President spoke at 9:05 p.m. in the House Chamber of the Capitol. He was introduced by Thomas P. O'Neill, Jr., Speaker of the House of Representatives. The address was broadcast live on nationwide radio and television.

THE STATE OF THE UNION

The State of the Union on February 4, 1986

Mr. Speaker, Mr. President, distinguished Members of the Congress, honored guests, and fellow citizens:

Thank you for allowing me to delay my address until this evening. We paused together to mourn and honor the valor of our seven Challenger heroes. And I hope that we are now ready to do what they would want us to do: Go forward, America, and reach for the stars. We will never forget those brave seven, but we shall go forward.

Mr. Speaker, before I begin my prepared remarks, may I point out that tonight marks the 10th and last State of the Union Message that you've presided over. And on behalf of the American people, I want to salute you for your service to Congress and country. Here's to you!

I have come to review with you the progress of our nation, to speak of unfinished work, and to set our sights on the future. I am pleased to report the state of our Union is stronger than a year ago and growing stronger each day. Tonight we look out on a rising America, firm of heart, united in spirit, powerful in pride and patriotism. America is on the move! But it wasn't long ago that we looked out on a different land: locked factory gates, long gasoline lines, intolerable prices, and interest rates turning the greatest country on Earth into a land of broken dreams.

Government growing beyond our consent had become a lumbering giant, slamming shut the gates of opportunity, threatening to crush the very roots of our freedom. What brought America back? The American people brought us back with quiet courage and common sense, with undying faith that in this nation under God the future will be ours; for the future belongs to the free.

Tonight the American people deserve our thanks for 37 straight months of economic growth, for sunrise firms and modernized industries creating 9 million new jobs in 3 years, interest rates cut in half, inflation falling over from 12 percent in 1980 to under 4 today, and a mighty river of good works-a record $74 billion in voluntary giving just last year alone. And despite the pressures of our modern world, family and community remain the moral core of our society, guardians of our values and hopes for the future. Family and community are the costars of this great American comeback. They are why we say tonight: Private values must be at the heart of public policies.

What is true for families in America is true for America in the family of free nations. History is no captive of some inevitable force. History is made by men and women of vision and courage. Tonight freedom is on the march. The United States is the economic miracle, the model to which the world once again turns. We stand for an idea whose time is now: Only by lifting the weights from the shoulders of all can people truly prosper and can peace among all nations be secure. Teddy Roosevelt said that a nation that does great work lives forever. We have done well, but we cannot stop at the foothills when Everest beckons. It's time for America to be all that we can be.

We speak tonight of an agenda for the future, an agenda for a safer, more secure world. And we speak about the necessity for actions to steel us for the challenges of growth, trade, and security in the next decade and the year 2000. And we will do it—not by breaking faith with bedrock principles but by breaking free from failed policies. Let us begin where storm clouds loom darkest—right here in Washington, DC. This week I will send you our detailed proposals; tonight let us speak of our responsibility to redefine government's role: not to control, not to demand or command, not to contain us, but to help in times of need and, above all, to create a ladder of opportunity to full employment so that all Americans can climb toward economic power and justice on their own.

But we cannot win the race to the future shackled to a system that can't even pass a Federal budget. We cannot win that race held back by horse-and-buggy programs that waste tax dollars and squander human potential. We cannot win that race if we're swamped in a sea of red ink. Now, Mr. Speaker, you know, I know, and the American people know the Federal budget system is broken. It doesn't work. Before we leave this city, let's you and I work together to fix it, and then we can finally give the American people a balanced budget.

Members of Congress, passage of Gramm-Rudman-Hollings gives us an historic opportunity to achieve what has eluded our national leadership for decades: forcing the Federal Government to live within its means. Your schedule now requires that the budget resolution be passed by April 15th, the very day America's families have to foot the bill for the budgets that you produce. How often we read of a husband and wife both working, struggling from paycheck to paycheck to raise a family, meet a mortgage, pay their taxes and bills. And yet some in Congress say taxes must be raised. Well, I'm sorry; they're asking the wrong people to tighten their belts. It's time we reduce the Federal budget and left the family budget alone. We do not face large deficits because American families are under taxed; we face those deficits because the Federal Government overspends.

The detailed budget that we will submit will meet the Gramm-Rudman-Hollings target for deficit reductions, meet our commitment to ensure a strong national defense, meet our commitment to protect Social Security and the truly less fortunate, and, yes, meet our commitment to not raise taxes. How should we accomplish this? Well, not by taking from those in need. As families take care of their own, government must provide shelter and nourishment for those who cannot provide for themselves. But we must revise or replace programs enacted in the name of compassion that degrade the moral worth of work, encourage family breakups, and drive entire communities into a bleak and heartless dependency. Gramm-Rudman-Hollings can mark a dramatic improvement. But experience shows that simply setting deficit targets does not assure they'll be met. We must proceed with Grace commission reforms against waste.

And tonight I ask you to give me what 43 Governors have: Give me a line-item veto this year. Give me the authority to veto waste, and I'll take the responsibility, I'll make the cuts, I'll take the heat. This authority would not give me any monopoly power, but simply prevent spending measures from sneaking through that could not pass on their own merit. And you can sustain or override my veto; that's the way the system should work. Once we've made the hard choices, we should lock in our gains with a balanced budget amendment to the Constitution.

I mentioned that we will meet our commitment to national defense. We must meet it. Defense is not just another budget expense. Keeping America strong, free, and at peace is solely the responsibility of the Federal Government; it is government's prime responsibility. We have devoted 5 years trying to narrow a dangerous gap born of illusion and neglect, and we've made important gains. Yet the threat from Soviet forces, conventional and strategic, from the Soviet drive for domination, from the increase in espionage and state terror remains great. This is reality. Closing our eyes will not make reality disappear. We pledged together to hold real growth in defense spending to the bare minimum. My budget honors that pledge, and I'm now asking you, the Congress, to keep its end of the bargain. The Soviets must know that if America reduces her defenses, it will be because of a reduced threat, not a reduced resolve.

Keeping America strong is as vital to the national security as controlling Federal spending is to our economic security. But, as I have said before, the most powerful force we can enlist against the Federal deficit is an ever-expanding American economy, unfettered and free. The magic of opportunity-unreserved, unfailing, unrestrained-isn't this the calling that unites us? I believe our tax rate cuts for the people have done more to spur a spirit of risk-taking and help America's economy break free than any program since John Kennedy's tax cut almost a quarter century ago.

Now history calls us to press on, to complete efforts for an historic tax reform providing new opportunity for all and ensuring that all pay their fair share, but no more. We've come this far. Will you join me now, and we'll walk this last mile together? You know my views on this. We cannot and we will not accept tax reform that is a tax increase in disguise. True reform must be an engine of productivity and growth, and that means a top personal rate no higher than 35 percent. True reform must be truly fair, and that means raising personal exemptions to $2,000. True reform means a tax system that at long last is pro-family, pro-jobs, pro-future, and pro-America.

As we knock down the barriers to growth, we must redouble our efforts for freer and fairer trade. We have already taken actions to counter unfair trading practices and to pry open closed foreign markets. We will continue to do so. We will also oppose legislation touted as providing protection that in reality pits one American worker against another, one industry against another, one community against another, and that raises prices for us all. If the United States can trade with other nations on a level playing field, we can out produce, out compete, and outsell anybody, anywhere in the world.

The constant expansion of our economy and exports requires a sound and stable dollar at home and reliable exchange rates around the world. We must never again permit wild currency swings to cripple our farmers and other exporters. Farmers, in particular, have suffered from past unwise government policies. They must not be abandoned with problems they did not create and cannot control. We've begun coordinating economic and monetary policy among our major trading partners. But there's more to do, and tonight I am directing Treasury Secretary Jim Baker to determine if the nations of the world should convene to discuss the role and relationship of our currencies.

Confident in our future and secure in our values, Americans are striving forward to embrace the future. We see it not only in our recovery but in 3 straight years of falling crime rates, as families and communities band together to fight pornography, drugs, and lawlessness and to give back to their children the safe and, yes, innocent childhood they deserve. We see it in the renaissance in education, the rising SAT scores for 3 years—last year's increase, the greatest since 1963. It wasn't government and Washington lobbies that turned education around; it was the American people who, in reaching for excellence, knew to reach back to basics. We must continue the advance by supporting discipline in our schools, vouchers that give parents freedom of choice; and we must give back to our children their lost right to acknowledge God in their classrooms.

We are a nation of idealists, yet today there is a wound in our national conscience. America will never be whole as long as the right to life granted by our Creator is denied to the unborn. For the rest of my time, I shall do what I can to see that this wound is one day healed.

As we work to make the American dream real for all, we must also look to the condition of America's families. Struggling parents today worry how they will provide their children the advantages that their parents gave them. In the welfare culture, the breakdown of the family, the most basic support system, has reached crisis proportions---'m female and child poverty, child abandonment, horrible crimes, and deteriorating schools.   After hundreds of billions of dollars in poverty programs, the plight of the poor grows more painful. But the waste in dollars and cents pales before the most tragic loss: the sinful waste of human spirit and potential. We can ignore this terrible truth no longer. As Franklin Roosevelt warned 51 years ago, standing before this Chamber, he said, "Welfare is a narcotic, a subtle destroyer of the human spirit." And we must now escape the spider's web of dependency.

Tonight I am charging the White House Domestic Council to present me by December 1, 1986, an evaluation of programs and a strategy for immediate action to meet the financial, educational, social, and safety concerns of poor families. I'm talking about real and lasting emancipation, because the success of welfare should be judged by how many of its recipients become independent of welfare. Further, after seeing how devastating illness can destroy the financial security of the family, I am directing the Secretary of Health and Human Services, Dr. Otis Bowen, to report to me by year end with recommendations on how the private sector and government can work together to address the problems of affordable insurance for those whose life savings would otherwise be threatened when catastrophic illness strikes.

And tonight I want to speak directly to America's younger generation, because you hold the destiny of our nation in your hands. With all the temptations young people face, it sometimes seems the allure of the permissive society requires superhuman feats of self-control. But the call of the future is too strong, the challenge too great to get lost in the blind alleyways of dissolution, drugs, and despair. Never has there been a more exciting time to be alive, a time of rousing wonder and heroic achievement. As they said in the film "Back to the Future," "Where we're going, we don't need roads."

Well, today physicists peering into the infinitely small realms of subatomic particles find reaffirmations of religious faith. Astronomers build a space telescope that can see to the edge of the universe and possibly back to the moment of creation. So, yes, this nation remains fully committed to America's space program. We're going forward with our shuttle flights. We're going forward to build our space station. And we are going forward with research on a new Orient Express that could, by the end of the next decade, take off from Dulles Airport, accelerate up to 25 times the speed of sound, attaining low Earth orbit or flying to Tokyo within 2 hours. And the same technology transforming our lives can solve the greatest problem of the 20th century. A security shield can one day render nuclear weapons obsolete and free mankind from the prison of nuclear terror. America met one historic challenge and went to the Moon. Now America must meet another: to make our strategic defense real for all the citizens of planet Earth.

Let us speak of our deepest longing for the future: to leave our children a land that is free and just and a world at peace. It is my hope that our fireside summit in Geneva and Mr. Gorbachev's upcoming visit to America can lead to a more stable relationship. Surely no people on Earth hate war or love peace more than we Americans. But we cannot stroll into the future with childlike faith. Our differences with a system that openly proclaims and practices an alleged right to command people's lives and to export its ideology by force are deep and abiding. Logic and history compel us to accept that our relationship be guided by realism—rock-hard, clear-eyed, steady, and sure. Our negotiators in Geneva have proposed a radical cut in offensive forces by each side with no cheating. They have made clear that Soviet compliance with the letter and spirit of agreements is essential. If the Soviet Government wants an agreement that truly reduces nuclear arms, there will be such an agreement.

But arms control is no substitute for peace. We know that peace follows in freedom's path and conflicts erupt when the will of the people is denied. So, we must prepare for peace not only by reducing weapons but by bolstering prosperity, liberty, and democracy however and wherever we can. We advance the promise of opportunity every time we speak out on behalf of lower tax rates, freer markets, sound currencies around the world. We strengthen the family of freedom every time we work with allies and come to the aid of friends under siege. And we can enlarge the family of free nations if we will defend the unalienable rights of all God's children to follow their dreams.

To those imprisoned in regimes held captive, to those beaten for daring to fight for freedom and democracy—for their right to worship, to speak, to live, and to prosper in the family of free nations—we say to you tonight:

You are not alone, freedom fighters. America will support with moral and material assistance your right not just to fight and die for freedom but to fight and win freedom—to win freedom in Afghanistan, in Angola, in Cambodia, and in Nicaragua. This is a great moral challenge for the entire free world.

Surely no issue is more important for peace in our own hemisphere, for the security of our frontiers, for the protection of our vital interests, than to achieve democracy in Nicaragua and to protect Nicaragua's democratic neighbors. This year I will be asking Congress for the means to do what must be done for that great and good cause. As (former Senator Henry M.)Scoop Jackson, the inspiration for our Bipartisan Commission on Central America, once said, "In matters of national security, the best politics is no politics."

What we accomplish this year, in each challenge we face, will set our course for the balance of the decade, indeed, for the remainder of the century. After all we've done so far, let no one say that this nation cannot reach the destiny of our dreams. America believes, America is ready, America can win the race to the future—and we shall. The American dream is a song of hope that rings through night winter air; vivid, tender music that warms our hearts when the least among us aspire to the greatest things: to venture a daring enterprise; to unearth new beauty in music, literature, and art; to discover a new universe inside a tiny silicon chip or a single human cell.

We see the dream coming true in the spirit of discovery of Richard Cavoli. All his life he's been enthralled by the mysteries of medicine. And, Richard, we know that the experiment that you began in high school was launched and lost last week, yet your dream lives. And as long as it's real, work of noble note will yet be done, work that could reduce the harmful effects of x rays on patients and enable astronomers to view the golden gateways of the farthest stars.

We see the dream glow in the towering talent of a 12-year-old, Tyrone Ford. A child prodigy of gospel music, he has surmounted personal adversity to become an accomplished pianist and singer. He also directs the choirs of three churches and has performed at the Kennedy Center. With God as your composer, Tyrone, your music will be the music of angels.

We see the dream being saved by the courage of the 13-year-old Shelby Butler, honor student and member of her school's safety patrol. Seeing another girl freeze in terror before an out-of-control school bus, she risked her life and pulled her to safety. With bravery like yours, Shelby, America need never fear for our future.

And we see the dream born again in the joyful compassion of a 13 year old, Trevor Ferrell. Two years ago, age 11, watching men and women bedding down in abandoned doorways—on television he was watching—Trevor left his suburban Philadelphia home to bring blankets and food to the helpless and homeless. And now 250 people help him fulfill his nightly vigil. Trevor, yours is the living spirit of brotherly love.

Would you four stand up for a moment? Thank you, thank you. You are heroes of our hearts. We look at you and know it's true: In this land of dreams fulfilled, where greater dreams may be imagined, nothing is impossible, no victory is beyond our reach, no glory will ever be too great.

So, now it's up to us, all of us, to prepare America for that day when our work will pale before the greatness of America's champions in the 21st century. The world's hopes rest with America's future; America's hopes rest with us. So, let us go forward to create our world of tomorrow in faith, in unity, and in love.

God bless you, and God bless America. NOTE: The President spoke at 8:04 p.m. in the House Chamber of the Capitol. He was introduced by Thomas P. O'Neill, Jr., Speaker of the House of Representatives. The address was broadcast live on nationwide radio and television.

THE STATE OF THE UNION

The State of the Union on January 27, 1987

Mr. Speaker, Mr. President, distinguished Members of Congress, honored guests, and fellow citizens:

May I congratulate all of you who are Members of this historic 100th Congress of the United States of America. In this 200th anniversary year of our Constitution, you and I stand on the shoulders of giants—men whose words and deeds put wind in the sails of freedom. However, we must always remember that our Constitution is to be celebrated not for being old, but for being young—young with the same energy, spirit, and promise that filled each eventful day in Philadelphia's statehouse. We will be guided tonight by their acts, and we will be guided forever by their words.

Now, forgive me, but I can't resist sharing a story from those historic days. Philadelphia was bursting with civic pride in the spring of 1787, and its newspapers began embellishing the arrival of the Convention delegates with elaborate social classifications. Governors of States were called Excellency. Justices and Chancellors had reserved for them honorable with a capital "H." For Congressmen, it was honorable with a small "h." And all others were referred to as "the following respectable characters." Well, for this 100th Congress, I invoke special executive powers to declare that each of you must never be titled less than honorable with a capital "H." Incidentally, I'm delighted you are celebrating the 100th birthday of the Congress. It's always a pleasure to congratulate someone with more birthdays than I've had.

Now, there's a new face at this place of honor tonight. And please join me in warm congratulations to the Speaker of the House, Jim Wright. Mr. Speaker, you might recall a similar situation in your very first session of Congress 32 years ago. Then, as now, the speakership had changed hands and another great son of Texas, Sam Rayburn—"Mr. Sam"—sat in your chair. I cannot find better words than those used by President Eisenhower that evening. He said, "We shall have much to do together; I am sure that we will get it done and that we shall do it in harmony and good will." Tonight I renew that pledge. To you, Mr. Speaker, and to Senate Majority Leader Robert Byrd, who brings 34 years of distinguished service to the Congress, may I say: Though there are changes in the Congress, America's interests remain the same. And I am confident that, along with Republican leaders Bob Michel and Bob Dole, this Congress can make history.

Six years ago I was here to ask the Congress to join me in America's new beginning. Well, the results are something of which we can all be proud. Our inflation rate is now the lowest in a quarter of a century. The prime interest rate has fallen from the 21 ½ percent the month before we took office to 7 ½ percent today. And those rates have triggered the most housing starts in 8 years. The unemployment rate—still too high—is the lowest in nearly 7 years, and our people have created nearly 13 million new jobs. Over 61 percent of everyone over the age of 16, male and female, is employed—the highest percentage on record. Let's roll up our sleeves and go to work and put America's economic engine at full throttle. We can also be heartened by our progress across the world. Most important, America is at peace tonight, and freedom is on the march. And we've done much these past years to restore our defenses, our alliances, and our leadership in the world. Our sons and daughters in the services once again wear their uniforms with pride.

But though we've made much progress, I have one major regret: I took a risk with regard to our action in Iran. It did not work, and for that I assume full responsibility. The goals were worthy. I do not believe it was wrong to try to establish contacts with a country of strategic importance or to try to save lives. And certainly it was not wrong to try to secure freedom for our citizens held in barbaric captivity. But we did not achieve what we wished, and serious mistakes were made in trying to do so. We will get to the bottom of this, and I will take whatever action is called for. But in debating the past, we must not deny ourselves the successes of the future. Let it never be said of this generation of Americans that we became so obsessed with failure that we refused to take risks that could further the cause of peace and freedom in the world. Much is at stake here, and the Nation and the world are watching to see if we go forward together in the national interest or if we let partisanship weaken us. And let there be no mistake about American policy: We will not sit idly by if our interests or our friends in the Middle East are threatened, nor will we yield to terrorist blackmail.

And now, ladies and gentlemen of the Congress, why don't we get to work? I am pleased to report that because of our efforts to rebuild the strength of America, the world is a safer place. Earlier this month I submitted a budget to defend America and maintain our momentum to make up for neglect in the last decade. Well, I ask you to vote out a defense and foreign affairs budget that says yes to protecting our country. While the world is safer, it is not safe.

Since 1970 the Soviets have invested $500 billion more on their military forces than we have. Even today, though nearly 1 in 3 Soviet families is without running hot water and the average family spends 2 hours a day shopping for the basic necessities of life, their government still found the resources to transfer $75 billion in weapons to client states in the past 5 years—clients like Syria, Vietnam, Cuba, Libya, Angola, Ethiopia, Afghanistan, and Nicaragua. With 120,000 Soviet combat and military personnel and 15,000 military advisers in Asia, Africa, and Latin America, can anyone still doubt their single-minded determination to expand their power? Despite this, the Congress cut my request for critical U.S. security assistance to free nations by 21 percent this year, and cut defense requests by $85 billion in the last 3 years.

These assistance programs serve our national interests as well as mutual interests. And when the programs are devastated, American interests are harmed. My friends, it's my duty as President to say to you again tonight that there is no surer way to lose freedom than to lose our resolve. Today the brave people of Afghanistan are showing that resolve. The Soviet Union says it wants a peaceful settlement in Afghanistan, yet it continues a brutal war and props up a regime whose days are clearly numbered. We are ready to support a political solution that guarantees the rapid withdrawal of all Soviet troops and genuine self-determination for the Afghan people.

In Central America, too, the cause of freedom is being tested. And our resolve is being tested there as well. Here, especially, the world is watching to see how this nation responds. Today over 90 percent of the people of Latin America live in democracy. Democracy is on the march in Central and South America. Communist Nicaragua is the odd man out—suppressing the church, the press, and democratic dissent and promoting subversion in the region. We support diplomatic efforts, but these efforts can never succeed if the Sandinistas win their war against the Nicaraguan people.

Our commitment to a Western Hemisphere safe from aggression did not occur by spontaneous generation on the day that we took office. It began with the Monroe Doctrine in 1823 and continues our historic bipartisan American policy. Franklin Roosevelt said we "are determined to do everything possible to maintain peace on this hemisphere." President Truman was very blunt: "International communism seeks to crush and undermine and destroy the independence of the Americas. We cannot let that happen here." And John F. Kennedy made clear that "Communist domination in this hemisphere can never be negotiated."

Some in this Congress may choose to depart from this historic commitment, but I will not.

This year we celebrate the second century of our Constitution. The Sandinistas just signed theirs 2 weeks ago, and then suspended it. We won't know how my words tonight will be reported there for one simple reason:

There is no free press in Nicaragua. Nicaraguan freedom fighters have never asked us to wage their battle, but I will fight any effort to shut off their lifeblood and consign them to death, defeat, or a life without freedom. There must be no Soviet beachhead in Central America.

You know, we Americans have always preferred dialog to conflict, and so, we always remain open to more constructive relations with the Soviet Union. But more responsible Soviet conduct around the world is a key element of the U.S.-Soviet agenda. Progress is also required on the other items of our agenda as well—real respect for human rights and more open contacts between our societies and, of course, arms reduction.

In Iceland, last October, we had one moment of opportunity that the Soviets dashed because they sought to cripple our Strategic Defense Initiative, SDI. I wouldn't let them do it then; I won't let them do it now or in the future. This is the most positive and promising defense program we have undertaken. It's the path, for both sides, to a safer future—a system that defends human life instead of threatening it. SDI will go forward. The United States has made serious, fair, and far-reaching proposals to the Soviet Union, and this is a moment of rare opportunity for arms reduction. But I will need, and American negotiators in Geneva will need, Congress' support. Enacting the Soviet negotiating position into American law would not be the way to win a good agreement. So, I must tell you in this Congress I will veto any effort that undercuts our national security and our negotiating leverage.

Now, today, we also find ourselves engaged in expanding peaceful commerce across the world. We will work to expand our opportunities in international markets through the Uruguay round of trade negotiations and to complete an historic free trade arrangement between the world's two largest trading partners, Canada and the United States. Our basic trade policy remains the same: We remain opposed as ever to protectionism, because America's growth and future depend on trade. But we would insist on trade that is fair and free. We are always willing to be trade partners but never trade patsies.

Now, from foreign borders let us return to our own, because America in the world is only as strong as America at home. This 100th Congress has high responsibilities. I begin with a gentle reminder that many of these are simply the incomplete obligations of the past. The American people deserve to be impatient, because we do not yet have the public house in order. We've had great success in restoring our economic integrity, and we've rescued our nation from the worst economic mess since the Depression. But there's more to do. For starters, the Federal deficit is outrageous. For years I've asked that we stop pushing onto our children the excesses of our government. And what the Congress finally needs to do is pass a constitutional amendment that mandates a balanced budget and forces government to live within its means. States, cities, and the families of America balance their budgets. Why can't we?

Next, the budget process is a sorry spectacle. The missing of deadlines and the nightmare of monstrous continuing resolutions packing hundreds of billions of dollars of spending into one bill must be stopped. We ask the Congress once again: Give us the same tool that 43 Governors have—a lineitem veto so we can carve out the boondoggles and pork, those items that would never survive on their own. I will send the Congress broad recommendations on the budget, but first I'd like to see yours. Let's go to work and get this done together.

But now let's talk about this year's budget. Even though I have submitted it within the Gramm-Rudman-Hollings deficit reduction target, I have seen suggestions that we might postpone that timetable. Well, I think the American people are tired of hearing the same old excuses. Together we made a commitment to balance the budget. Now let's keep it. As for those suggestions that the answer is higher taxes, the American people have repeatedly rejected that shop-worn advice. They know that we don't have deficits because people are taxed too little. We have deficits because big government spends too much.

Now, next month I'll place two additional reforms before the Congress. We've created a welfare monster that is a shocking indictment of our sense of priorities. Our national welfare system consists of some 59 major programs and over 6,000 pages of Federal laws and regulations on which more than $132 billion was spent in 1985. I will propose a new national welfare strategy, a program of welfare reform through State-sponsored, community-based demonstration projects. This is the time to reform this outmoded social dinosaur and finally break the poverty trap. Now, we will never abandon those who, through no fault of their own, must have our help. But let us work to see how many can be freed from the dependency of welfare and made self-supporting, which the great majority of welfare recipients want more than anything else. Next, let us remove a financial specter facing our older Americans: the fear of an illness so expensive that it can result in having to make an intolerable choice between bankruptcy and death. I will submit legislation shortly to help free the elderly from the fear of catastrophic illness.

Now let's turn to the future. It's widely said that America is losing her competitive edge. Well, that won't happen if we act now. How well prepared are we to enter the 21st century? In my lifetime, America set the standard for the world. It is now time to determine that we should enter the next century having achieved a level of excellence unsurpassed in history. We will achieve this, first, by guaranteeing that government does everything possible to promote America's ability to compete. Second, we must act as individuals in a quest for excellence that will not be measured by new proposals or billions in new funding. Rather, it involves an expenditure of American spirit and just plain American grit. The Congress will soon receive my comprehensive proposals to enhance our competitiveness, including new science and technology centers and strong new funding for basic research. The bill will include legal and regulatory reforms and weapons to fight unfair trade practices. Competitiveness also means giving our farmers a shot at participating fairly and fully in a changing world market.

Preparing for the future must begin, as always, with our children. We need to set for them new and more rigorous goals. We must demand more of ourselves and our children by raising literacy levels dramatically by the year 2000. Our children should master the basic concepts of math and science, and let's insist that students not leave high school until they have studied and understood the basic documents of our national heritage. There's one more thing we can't let up on: Let's redouble our personal efforts to provide for every child a safe and drug-free learning environment. If our crusade against drugs succeeds with our children, we will defeat that scourge all over the country.

Finally, let's stop suppressing the spiritual core of our national being. Our nation could not have been conceived without divine help. Why is it that we can build a nation with our prayers, but we can't use a schoolroom for voluntary prayer? The 100th Congress of the United States should be remembered as the one that ended the expulsion of God from America's classrooms.

The quest for excellence into the 21st century begins in the schoolroom but must go next to the workplace. More than 20 million new jobs will be created before the new century unfolds, and by then, our economy should be able to provide a job for everyone who wants to work. We must also enable our workers to adapt to the rapidly changing nature of the workplace. And I will propose substantial, new Federal commitments keyed to retraining and job mobility.

Over the next few weeks, I'll be sending the Congress a complete series of these special messages—on budget reform, welfare reform, competitiveness, including education, trade, worker training and assistance, agriculture, and other subjects. The Congress can give us these tools, but to make these tools work, it really comes down to just being our best. And that is the core of American greatness. The responsibility of freedom presses us towards higher knowledge and, I believe, moral and spiritual greatness. Through lower taxes and smaller government, government has its ways of freeing people's spirits. But only we, each of us, can let the spirit soar against our own individual standards. Excellence is what makes freedom ring. And isn't that what we do best?

We're entering our third century now, but it's wrong to judge our nation by its years. The calendar can't measure America because we were meant to be an endless experiment in freedom—with no limit to our reaches, no boundaries to what we can do, no end point to our hopes. The United States Constitution is the impassioned and inspired vehicle by which we travel through history. It grew out of the most fundamental inspiration of our existence: that we are here to serve Him by living free—that living free releases in us the noblest of impulses and the best of our abilities; that we would use these gifts for good and generous purposes and would secure them not just for ourselves and for our children but for all mankind.

Over the years—I won't count if you don't—nothing has been so heartwarming to me as speaking to America's young, and the little ones especially, so fresh-faced and so eager to know. Well, from time to time I've been with them—they will ask about our Constitution. And I hope you Members of Congress will not deem this a breach of protocol if you'll permit me to share these thoughts again with the young people who might be listening or watching this evening. I've read the constitutions of a number of countries, including the Soviet Union's. Now, some people are surprised to hear that they have a constitution, and it even supposedly grants a number of freedoms to its people. Many countries have written into their constitution provisions for freedom of speech and freedom of assembly. Well, if this is true, why is the Constitution of the United States so exceptional?

Well, the difference is so small that it almost escapes you, but it's so great it tells you the whole story in just three words: We the people. In those other constitutions, the Government tells the people of those countries what they're allowed to do. In our Constitution, we the people tell the Government what it can do, and it can do only those things listed in that document and no others. Virtually every other revolution in history has just exchanged one set of rulers for another set of rulers. Our revolution is the first to say the people are the masters and government is their servant. And you young people out there, don't ever forget that. Someday you could be in this room, but wherever you are, America is depending on you to reach your highest and be your best—because here in America, we the people are in charge.

Just three words: We the people—those are the kids on Christmas Day looking out from a frozen sentry post on the 38th parallel in Korea or aboard an aircraft carrier in the Mediterranean. A million miles from home, but doing their duty.

We the people—those are the warmhearted whose numbers we can't begin to count, who'll begin the day with a little prayer for hostages they will never know and MIA families they will never meet. Why? Because that's the way we are, this unique breed we call Americans.

We the people—they're farmers on tough times, but who never stop feeding a hungry world. They're the volunteers at the hospital choking back their tears for the hundredth time, caring for a baby struggling for life because of a mother who used drugs. And you'll forgive me a special memory—it's a million mothers like Nelle Reagan who never knew a stranger or turned a hungry person away from her kitchen door.

We the people—they refute last week's television commentary downgrading our optimism and our idealism. They are the entrepreneurs, the builders, the pioneers, and a lot of regular folks—the true heroes of our land who make up the most uncommon nation of doers in history. You know they're Americans because their spirit is as big as the universe and their hearts are bigger than their spirits.

We the people—starting the third century of a dream and standing up to some cynic who's trying to tell us we're not going to get any better. Are we at the end? Well, I can't tell it any better than the real thing—a story recorded by James Madison from the final moments of the Constitutional Convention, September 17th, 1787. As the last few members signed the document, Benjamin Franklin—the oldest delegate at 81 years and in frail health—looked over toward the chair where George Washington daily presided. At the back of the chair was painted the picture of a Sun on the horizon. And turning to those sitting next to him, Franklin observed that artists found it difficult in their painting to distinguish between a rising and a setting Sun.

Well, I know if we were there, we could see those delegates sitting around Franklin-leaning in to listen more closely to him. And then Dr. Franklin began to share his deepest hopes and fears about the outcome of their efforts, and this is what he said: "I have often looked at that picture behind the President without being able to tell whether it was a rising or setting Sun: But now at length I have the happiness to know that it is a rising and not a setting Sun." Well, you can bet it's rising because, my fellow citizens, America isn't finished. Her best days have just begun.

Thank you, God bless you, and God bless America. NOTE: The President spoke at 9:03 p.m. in the House Chamber of the Capitol. He was introduced by Jim Wright, Speaker of the House of Representatives. The address was broadcast live on nationwide radio and television.

The State of the Union on January 25, 1988

Mr. Speaker, Mr. President, and distinguished Members of the House and Senate: When we first met here 7 years ago-many of us for the first time—it was with the hope of beginning something new for America. We meet here tonight in this historic Chamber to continue that work. If anyone expects just a proud recitation of the accomplishments of my administration, I say let's leave that to history; we're not finished yet. So, my message to you tonight is put on your work shoes; we're still on the job.

History records the power of the ideas that brought us here those 7 years ago-ideas like the individual's right to reach as far and as high as his or her talents will permit; the free market as an engine of economic progress. And as an ancient Chinese philosopher, Lao-tzu, said: "Govern a great nation as you would cook a small fish; do not overdo it." Well, these ideas were part of a larger notion, a vision, if you will, of America herself---an America not only rich in opportunity for the individual but an America, too, of strong families and vibrant neighborhoods; an America whose divergent but harmonizing communities were a reflection of a deeper community of values: the value of work, of family, of religion, and of the love of freedom that God places in each of us and whose defense He has entrusted in a special way to this nation.

All of this was made possible by an idea I spoke of when Mr. Gorbachev was here-the belief that the most exciting revolution ever known to humankind began with three simple words: "We the People," the revolutionary notion that the people grant government its rights, and not the other way around. And there's one lesson that has come home powerfully to me, which I would offer to you now. Just as those who created this Republic pledged to each other their lives, their fortunes, and their sacred honor, so, too, America's leaders today must pledge to each other that we will keep foremost in our hearts and minds not what is best for ourselves or for our party but what is best for America.

In the spirit of Jefferson, let us affirm that in this Chamber tonight there are no Republicans, no Democrats—just Americans. Yes, we will have our differences, but let us always remember what unites us far outweighs whatever divides us. Those who sent us here to serve them—the millions of Americans watching and listening tonight-expect this of us. Let's prove to them and to ourselves that democracy works even in an election year. We've done this before. And as we have worked together to bring down spending, tax rates, and inflation, employment has climbed to record heights; America has created more jobs and better, higher paying jobs; family income has risen for 4 straight years, and America's poor climbed out of poverty at the fastest rate in more than 10 years.

Our record is not just the longest peacetime expansion in history but an economic and social revolution of hope based on work, incentives, growth, and opportunity; a revolution of compassion that led to private sector initiatives and a 77-percent increase in charitable giving; a revolution that at a critical moment in world history reclaimed and restored the American dream.

In international relations, too, there's only one description for what, together, we have achieved: a complete turnabout, a revolution. Seven years ago, America was weak, and freedom everywhere was under siege. Today America is strong, and democracy is everywhere on the move. From Central America to East Asia, ideas like free markets and democratic reforms and human rights are taking hold. We've replaced "Blame America" with "Look up to America." We've rebuilt our defenses. And of all our accomplishments, none can give us more satisfaction than knowing that our young people are again proud to wear our country's uniform.

And in a few moments, I'm going to talk about three developments—arms reduction, the Strategic Defense Initiative, and the global democratic revolution—that, when taken together, offer a chance none of us would have dared imagine 7 years ago, a chance to rid the world of the two great nightmares of the postwar era. I speak of the startling hope of giving our children a future free of both totalitarianism and nuclear terror.

Tonight, then, we're strong, prosperous, at peace, and we are free. This is the state of our Union. And if we will work together this year, I believe we can give a future President and a future Congress the chance to make that prosperity, that peace, that freedom not just the state of our Union but the state of our world.

Toward this end, we have four basic objectives tonight. First, steps we can take this year to keep our economy strong and growing, to give our children a future of low inflation and full employment. Second, let's check our progress in attacking social problems, where important gains have been made, but which still need critical attention. I mean schools that work, economic independence for the poor, restoring respect for family life and family values. Our third objective tonight is global: continuing the exciting economic and democratic revolutions we've seen around the world. Fourth and finally, our nation has remained at peace for nearly a decade and a half, as we move toward our goals of world prosperity and world freedom. We must protect that peace and deter war by making sure the next President inherits what you and I have a moral obligation to give that President: a national security that is unassailable and a national defense that takes full advantage of new technology and is fully funded.

This is a full agenda. It's meant to be. You see, my thinking on the next year is quite simple: Let's make this the best of 8. And that means it's all out—right to the finish line. I don't buy the idea that this is the last year of anything, because we're not talking here tonight about registering temporary gains but ways of making permanent our successes. And that's why our focus is the values, the principles, and ideas that made America great. Let's be clear on this point. We're for limited government, because we understand, as the Founding Fathers did, that it is the best way of ensuring personal liberty and empowering the individual so that every American of every race and region shares fully in the flowering of American prosperity and freedom.

One other thing we Americans like—the future—like the sound of it, the idea of it, the hope of it. Where others fear trade and economic growth, we see opportunities for creating new wealth and undreamed-of opportunities for millions in our own land and beyond. Where others seek to throw up barriers, we seek to bring them down. Where others take counsel of their fears, we follow our hopes. Yes, we Americans like the future and like making the most of it. Let's do that now.

And let's begin by discussing how to maintain economic growth by controlling and eventually eliminating the problem of Federal deficits. We have had a balanced budget only eight times in the last 57 years. For the first time in 14 years, the Federal Government spent less in real terms last year than the year before. We took $73 billion off last year's deficit compared to the year before. The deficit itself has moved from 6.3 percent of the gross national product to only 3.4 percent. And perhaps the most important sign of progress has been the change in our view of deficits. You know, a few of us can remember when, not too many years ago, those who created the deficits said they would make us prosperous and not to worry about the debt, because we owe it to ourselves. Well, at last there is agreement that we can't spend ourselves rich.

Our recent budget agreement, designed to reduce Federal deficits by $76 billion over the next 2 years, builds on this consensus. But this agreement must be adhered to without slipping into the errors of the past: more broken promises and more unchecked spending. As I indicated in my first State of the Union, what ails us can be simply put: The Federal Government is too big, and it spends too much money. I can assure you, the bipartisan leadership of Congress, of my help in fighting off any attempt to bust our budget agreement. And this includes the swift and certain use of the veto power.

Now, it's also time for some plain talk about the most immediate obstacle to controlling Federal deficits. The simple but frustrating problem of making expenses match revenues—something American families do and the Federal Government can't—has caused crisis after crisis in this city. Mr. Speaker, Mr. President, I will say to you tonight what I have said before and will continue to say: The budget process has broken down; it needs a drastic overhaul. With each ensuing year, the spectacle before the American people is the same as it was this Christmas: budget deadlines delayed or missed completely, monstrous continuing resolutions that pack hundreds of billions of dollars worth of spending into one bill, and a Federal Government on the brink of default.

I know I'm echoing what you here in the Congress have said, because you suffered so directly. But let's recall that in 7 years, of 91 appropriations bills scheduled to arrive on my desk by a certain date, only 10 made it on time. Last year, of the 13 appropriations bills due by October 1st, none of them made it. Instead, we had four continuing resolutions lasting 41 days, then 36 days, and 2 days, and 3 days, respectively.

And then, along came these behemoths. This is the conference report--1,053 pages, report weighing 14 pounds. Then this—a reconciliation bill 6 months late that was 1,186 pages long, weighing 15 pounds. And the long-term continuing resolution—this one was 2 months late, and it's 1,057 pages long, weighing 14 pounds. That was a total of 43 pounds of paper and ink. You had 3 hours—yes, 3 hours—to consider each, and it took 300 people at my Office of Management and Budget just to read the bill so the Government wouldn't shut down. Congress shouldn't send another one of these. No, and if you do, I will not sign it.

Let's change all this. Instead of a Presidential budget that gets discarded and a congressional budget resolution that is not enforced, why not a simple partnership, a joint agreement that sets out the spending priorities within the available revenues? And let's remember our deadline is October 1st, not Christmas. Let's get the people's work done in time to avoid a footrace with Santa Claus. And, yes, this year—to coin a phrase—a new beginning: 13 individual bills, on time and fully reviewed by Congress.

I'm also certain you join me in saying: Let's help ensure our future of prosperity by giving the President a tool that, though I will not get to use it, is one I know future Presidents of either party must have. Give the President the same authority that 43 Governors use in their States: the right to reach into massive appropriation bills, pare away the waste, and enforce budget discipline. Let's approve the line-item veto.

And let's take a partial step in this direction. Most of you in this Chamber didn't know what was in this catchall bill and report. Over the past few weeks, we've all learned what was tucked away behind a little comma here and there. For example, there's millions for items such as cranberry research, blueberry research, the study of crawfish, and the commercialization of wildflowers. And that's not to mention the five or so million ($.5 million) that—so that people from developing nations could come here to watch Congress at work. I won't even touch that. So, tonight I offer you this challenge. In 30 days I will send back to you those items as rescissions, which if I had the authority to line them out I would do so.

Now, review this multibillion-dollar package that will not undercut our bipartisan budget agreement. As a matter of fact, if adopted, it will improve our deficit reduction goals. And what an example we can set, that we're serious about getting our financial accounts in order. By acting and approving this plan, you have the opportunity to override a congressional process that is out of control.

There is another vital reform. Yes, Gramm-Rudman-Hollings has been profoundly helpful, but let us take its goal of a balanced budget and make it permanent. Let us do now what so many States do to hold down spending and what 32 State legislatures have asked us to do. Let us heed the wishes of an overwhelming plurality of Americans and pass a constitutional amendment that mandates a balanced budget and forces the Federal Government to live within its means. Reform of the budget process—including the line-item veto and balanced budget amendment—will, together with real restraint on government spending, prevent the Federal budget from ever again ravaging the family budget.

Let's ensure that the Federal Government never again legislates against the family and the home. Last September 1 signed an Executive order on the family requiring that every department and agency review its activities in light of seven standards designed to promote and not harm the family. But let us make certain that the family is always at the center of the public policy process not just in this administration but in all future administrations. It's time for Congress to consider, at the beginning, a statement of the impact that legislation will have on the basic unit of American society, the family.

And speaking of the family, let's turn to a matter on the mind of every American parent tonight: education. We all know the sorry story of the sixties and seventies-soaring spending, plummeting test scores-and that hopeful trend of the eighties, when we replaced an obsession with dollars with a commitment to quality, and test scores started back up. There's a lesson here that we all should write on the blackboard a hundred times: In a child's education, money can never take the place of basics like discipline, hard work, and, yes, homework.

As a nation we do, of course, spend heavily on education—more than we spend on defense. Yet across our country, Governors like New Jersey's Tom Kean are giving classroom demonstrations that how we spend is as important as how much we spend. Opening up the teaching profession to all qualified candidates, merit pay— so that good teachers get A's as well as apples—and stronger curriculum, as Secretary Bennett has proposed for high schools—these imaginative reforms are making common sense the most popular new kid in America's schools. How can we help? Well, we can talk about and push for these reforms. But the most important thing we can do is to reaffirm that control of our schools belongs to the States, local communities and, most of all, to the parents and teachers.

My friends, some years ago, the Federal Government declared war on poverty, and poverty won. Today the Federal Government has 59 major welfare programs and spends more than $100 billion a year on them. What has all this money done? Well, too often it has only made poverty harder to escape. Federal welfare programs have created a massive social problem. With the best of intentions, government created a poverty trap that wreaks havoc on the very support system the poor need most to lift themselves out of poverty: the family. Dependency has become the one enduring heirloom, passed from one generation to the next, of too many fragmented families.

It is time—this may be the most radical thing I've said in 7 years in this office—it's time for Washington to show a little humility. There are a thousand sparks of genius in 50 States and a thousand communities around the Nation. It is time to nurture them and see which ones can catch fire and become guiding lights. States have begun to show us the way. They've demonstrated that successful welfare programs can be built around more effective child support enforcement practices and innovative programs requiring welfare recipients to work or prepare for work. Let us give the States more flexibility and encourage more reforms. Let's start making our welfare system the first rung on America's ladder of opportunity, a boost up from dependency, not a graveyard but a birthplace of hope.

And now let me turn to three other matters vital to family values and the quality of family life. The first is an untold American success story. Recently, we released our annual survey of what graduating high school seniors have to say about drugs. Cocaine use is declining, and marijuana use was the lowest since surveying began. We can be proud that our students are just saying no to drugs. But let us remember what this menace requires: commitment from every part of America and every single American, a commitment to a drug free America. The war against drugs is a war of individual battles, a crusade with many heroes, including America's young people and also someone very special to me. She has helped so many of our young people to say no to drugs. Nancy, much credit belongs to you, and I want to express to you your husband's pride and your country's thanks.'. Surprised you, didn't I?

Well, now we come to a family issue that we must have the courage to confront. Tonight, I call America—a good nation, a moral people—to charitable but realistic consideration of the terrible cost of abortion on demand. To those who say this violates a woman's right to control of her own body: Can they deny that now medical evidence confirms the unborn child is a living human being entitled to life, liberty, and the pursuit of happiness? Let us unite as a nation and protect the unborn with legislation that would stop all Federal funding for abortion and with a human life amendment making, of course, an exception where the unborn child threatens the life of the mother. Our Judeo-Christian tradition recognizes the right of taking a life in self-defense. But with that one exception, let us look to those others in our land who cry out for children to adopt. I pledge to you tonight I will work to remove barriers to adoption and extend full sharing in family life to millions of Americans so that children who need homes can be welcomed to families who want them and love them.

And let me add here: So many of our greatest statesmen have reminded us that spiritual values alone are essential to our nation's health and vigor. The Congress opens its proceedings each day, as does the Supreme Court, with an acknowledgment of the Supreme Being. Yet we are denied the right to set aside in our schools a moment each day for those who wish to pray. I believe Congress should pass our school prayer amendment.

Now, to make sure there is a full nine member Supreme Court to interpret the law, to protect the rights of all Americans, I urge the Senate to move quickly and decisively in confirming Judge Anthony Kennedy to the highest Court in the land and to also confirm 27 nominees now waiting to fill vacancies in the Federal judiciary.

Here then are our domestic priorities. Yet if the Congress and the administration work together, even greater opportunities lie ahead to expand a growing world economy, to continue to reduce the threat of nuclear arms, and to extend the frontiers of freedom and the growth of democratic institutions.

Our policies consistently received the strongest support of the late Congressman Dan Daniel of Virginia. I'm sure all of you join me in expressing heartfelt condolences on his passing.

One of the greatest contributions the United States can make to the world is to promote freedom as the key to economic growth. A creative, competitive America is the answer to a changing world, not trade wars that would close doors, create greater barriers, and destroy millions of jobs. We should always remember: Protectionism is destructionism. America's jobs, America's growth, America's future depend on trade—trade that is free, open, and fair.

This year, we have it within our power to take a major step toward a growing global economy and an expanding cycle of prosperity that reaches to all the free nations of this Earth. I'm speaking of the historic free trade agreement negotiated between our country and Canada. And I can also tell you that we're determined to expand this concept, south as well as north. Next month I will be traveling to Mexico, where trade matters will be of foremost concern. And over the next several months, our Congress and the Canadian Parliament can make the start of such a North American accord a reality. Our goal must be a day when the free flow of trade, from the tip of Tierra del Fuego to the Arctic Circle, unites the people of the Western Hemisphere in a bond of mutually beneficial exchange, when all borders become what the U.S.-

Canadian border so long has been: a meeting place rather than a dividing line.

This movement we see in so many places toward economic freedom is indivisible from the worldwide movement toward political freedom and against totalitarian rule. This global democratic revolution has removed the specter, so frightening a decade ago, of democracy doomed to permanent minority status in the world. In South and Central America, only a third of the people enjoyed democratic rule in 1976. Today over 90 percent of Latin Americans live in nations committed to democratic principles. And the resurgence of democracy is owed to these courageous people on almost every continent who have struggled to take control of their own destiny.

In Nicaragua the struggle has extra meaning, because that nation is so near our own borders. The recent revelations of a former high-level Sandinista major, Roger Miranda, show us that, even as they talk peace, the Communist Sandinista government of Nicaragua has established plans for a large 600,000-man army. Yet even as these plans are made, the Sandinista regime knows the tide is turning, and the cause of Nicaraguan freedom is riding at its crest. Because of the freedom fighters, who are resisting Communist rule, the Sandinistas have been forced to extend some democratic rights, negotiate with church authorities, and release a few political prisoners.

The focus is on the Sandinistas, their promises and their actions. There is a consensus among the four Central American democratic Presidents that the Sandinistas have not complied with the plan to bring peace and democracy to all of Central America. The Sandinistas again have promised reforms. Their challenge is to take irreversible steps toward democracy. On Wednesday my request to sustain the freedom fighters will be submitted, which reflects our mutual desire for peace, freedom, and democracy in Nicaragua. I ask Congress to pass this request. Let us be for the people of Nicaragua what Lafayette, Pulaski, and Von Steuben were for our forefathers and the cause of American independence.

So, too, in Afghanistan, the freedom fighters are the key to peace. We support the Mujahidin. There can be no settlement unless all Soviet troops are removed and the Afghan people are allowed genuine self-determination. I have made my views on this matter known to Mr. Gorbachev. But not just Nicaragua or Afghanistan—yes, everywhere we see a swelling freedom tide across the world: freedom fighters rising up in Cambodia and Angola, fighting and dying for the same democratic liberties we hold sacred. Their cause is our cause: freedom.

Yet even as we work to expand world freedom, we must build a safer peace and reduce the danger of nuclear war. But let's have no illusions. Three years of steady decline in the value of our annual defense investment have increased the risk of our most basic security interests, jeopardizing earlier hard-won goals. We must face squarely the implications of this negative trend and make adequate, stable defense spending a top goal both this year and in the future.

This same concern applies to economic and security assistance programs as well. But the resolve of America and its NATO allies has opened the way for unprecedented achievement in arms reduction. Our recently signed INF treaty is historic, because it reduces nuclear arms and establishes the most stringent verification regime in arms control history, including several forms of short-notice, on-site inspection. I submitted the treaty today, and I urge the Senate to give its advice and consent to ratification of this landmark agreement. Thank you very much.

In addition to the INF treaty, we're within reach of an even more significant START agreement that will reduce U.S. and Soviet long-range missile—or strategic arsenals by half. But let me be clear. Our approach is not to seek agreement for agreement's sake but to settle only for agreements that truly enhance our national security and that of our allies. We will never put our security at risk—or that of our allies-just to reach an agreement with the Soviets. No agreement is better than a bad agreement.

As I mentioned earlier, our efforts are to give future generations what we never had—a future free of nuclear terror. Reduction of strategic offensive arms is one step, SDI another. Our funding request for our Strategic Defense Initiative is less than 2 percent of the total defense budget. SDI funding is money wisely appropriated and money well spent. SDI has the same purpose and supports the same goals of arms reduction. It reduces the risk of war and the threat of nuclear weapons to all mankind. Strategic defenses that threaten no one could offer the world a safer, more stable basis for deterrence. We must also remember that SDI is our insurance policy against a nuclear accident, a Chernobyl of the sky, or an accidental launch or some madman who might come along.

We've seen such changes in the world in 7 years. As totalitarianism struggles to avoid being overwhelmed by the forces of economic advance and the aspiration for human freedom, it is the free nations that are resilient and resurgent. As the global democratic revolution has put totalitarianism on the defensive, we have left behind the days of retreat. America is again a vigorous leader of the free world, a nation that acts decisively and firmly in the furtherance of her principles and vital interests. No legacy would make me more proud than leaving in place a bipartisan consensus for the cause of world freedom, a consensus that prevents a paralysis of American power from ever occurring again.

But my thoughts tonight go beyond this, and I hope you'll let me end this evening with a personal reflection. You know, the world could never be quite the same again after Jacob Shallus, a trustworthy and dependable clerk of the Pennsylvania General Assembly, took his pen and engrossed those words about representative government in the preamble of our Constitution. And in a quiet but final way, the course of human events was forever altered when, on a ridge overlooking the Emmitsburg Pike in an obscure Pennsylvania town called Gettysburg, Lincoln spoke of our duty to government of and by the people and never letting it perish from the Earth.

At the start of this decade, I suggested that we live in equally momentous times, that it is up to us now to decide whether our form of government would endure and whether history still had a place of greatness for a quiet, pleasant, greening land called America. Not everything has been made perfect in 7 years, nor will it be made perfect in seven times 70 years, but before us, this year and beyond, are great prospects for the cause of peace and world freedom.

It means, too, that the young Americans I spoke of 7 years ago, as well as those who might be coming along the Virginia or Maryland shores this night and seeing for the first time the lights of this Capital City—the lights that cast their glow on our great halls of government and the monuments to the memory of our great men—it means those young Americans will find a city of hope in a land that is free.

We can be proud that for them and for us, as those lights along the Potomac are still seen this night signaling as they have for nearly two centuries and as we pray God they always will, that another generation of Americans has protected and passed on lovingly this place called America, this shining city on a hill, this government of, by, and for the people.

Thank you, and God bless you. NOTE: The President spoke at 9:07 p.m. in the House Chamber of the Capitol. He was introduced by Jim Wright, Speaker of the House of Representatives. The address was broadcast live on nationwide radio and television.

Origins and authorization of the State of the Union Address

The formal basis for the State of the Union Address is from the U.S. Constitution:
- The President "shall from time to time give to the Congress Information on the State of the Union, and recommend to their Consideration such measures as he shall judge necessary and expedient." Article II, Section 3, Clause 1.

The constitutionally-mandated presidential address has gone through a few name changes:
- It was formally known as the Annual Message from 1790 to 1934.
- It began to be informally called the State of the Union Address from 1942 to 1946.
- Since 1947 it has generally been known as the State of the Union Address.

Earlier Annual Messages of the President included agency budget requests and general reports on the health of the economy. During the 20th century Congress required more specialized reports on these two aspects separate from the Annual Message.

- Budget Message, required by the National Budget and Accounting Act of 1921 (42 Stat. 20) to be delivered to Congress no more than two weeks after Congress convenes in January.
- Economic Report, required by the Employment Act of 1946 (60 Stat. 23), with a flexible delivery date.

Over time, as the message content changed, the focus of the State of the Union also changed:

- In the 19th century, the annual message was both a lengthy administrative report on the various departments of the executive and a budget and economic message.
- After 1913, when Woodrow Wilson revived the practice of presenting the message to Congress in person, it became a platform for the president to rally support for his agenda.
- Technological changes—radio, television, and the internet—further developed the State of the Union into a forum for the president to speak directly to the American people.

Where and when the State of the Union Address takes place

In modern practice, the State of the Union Message is delivered in the House Chamber. Prior to the move to the Capitol the Senate Chamber was often where the Annual Message was delivered by the president.

A House concurrent resolution sets aside the day and time for a joint session "for receiving such communication as the President of the United States shall be pleased to make to them" and is passed by both the House and Senate.

The ratification of the 20th Amendment on January 23, 1933 changed the opening of Congress from early March to early January, affecting the delivery of the Annual Message.

- Until 1934, the Message was delivered every December.
- Since 1934, the Message and Address is delivered every January or February.

THE STATE OF THE UNION

Attendance at the State of the Union

The following officials occupy floor seating in the House Chamber during the Address:

- Members and former Members of the House of Representative.
- Members and former Members of the Senate.
- The President's Cabinet, save one secretary, and the Joint Chiefs of Staff.
- The Chief Justice of the United States and the Justices of the Supreme Court.
- Diplomatic Corps.

Seating in the gallery is by tickets only, coordinated by the Sergeant-at-Arms of the House.

Since President Ronald Reagan's State of the Union Addresses, some personal guests of the president in the gallery have been publicly recognized in the course of the Address.

THE STATE OF THE UNION

Presidential delivery of the Annual Messages and State of the Union Addresses

- President George Washington combined the Inaugural Address with his Annual Message on April 30, 1789. He read the Address to a joint session of Congress in the Senate Chamber, Federal Hall, New York City. Washington delivered his first regular Annual Message to a joint session of Congress in New York City on January 8, 1790.
- President Thomas Jefferson began the practice of sending separate written Annual Messages to the House and Senate with his first one on December 8, 1801.
- President Woodrow Wilson revived the practice of delivering the Annual Message in person to a joint session of Congress on December 2, 1913, after delivering three special messages to Congress in person earlier in the year (tariff on April 8, currency and bank reform on June 23, and Mexican affairs on August 27).
- Presidents have occasionally sent a written Annual Message or State of the Union Address rather than deliver it in person. These include Presidents Woodrow Wilson (1919-1921), Calvin Coolidge (1924-1929), Herbert Hoover (1929-1933), Franklin Roosevelt (twice), Harry Truman (1946, 1953),

Dwight Eisenhower (1956, 1961), Richard Nixon (1973), Jimmy Carter (1981), and Ronald Reagan (1989).

- President Ronald Reagan's State of the Union Address for 1986 was rescheduled because of the *Challenger* disaster that took place earlier in the day.

Several recent Presidents have chosen not to send or deliver a formal State of the Union Address during their first year in office, preferring to deliver more special messages to Congress on various policies and topics:

- President Ronald Reagan on economic recovery, 1981.
- President George H.W. Bush on "Building a Better America," 1989.
- President William J. Clinton on the economy, 1993.
- President George W. Bush on the economy, 2001.

In a few cases, during a transition between administrations, there have been two State of the Union messages in a single year. In these cases, usually one message is in writing while the other is personally delivered by the President before a joint session of Congress:

- Presidents Harry Truman (written message) and Dwight Eisenhower (address before Congress), 1953.
- Presidents Dwight Eisenhower (written message) and John Kennedy (address before Congress), 1961.

Technology and the delivery of the Annual Messages and State of the Union Addresses

- First radio broadcast of Message: President Calvin Coolidge, 1923.

- First television broadcast of Message: President Harry Truman, 1947.

- First evening delivery of Message: President Lyndon Johnson, 1965.

- First live web cast on internet: President George W. Bush, 2002.

- First high definition television broadcast of Message, President George W. Bush, 2004.

THE STATE OF THE UNION

Historical highlights of the Annual Messages and State of the Union Addresses

- The longest: President Harry Truman, 1946, more than 25,000 words.
- The shortest: President George Washington, 1790, 833 words.
- Average length: 19th century was about 10,000 words; late-20th century, about 5000 words.
- Most Messages/Addresses given: President Franklin Roosevelt, 12 (10 were personal appearances before Congress).
- Fewest Messages/Address given: President Zachary Taylor, 1; President William Henry Harrison, 0; President James A. Garfield, 0.

THE STATE OF THE UNION

Response by the opposition party to the State of the Union Address

- Practice began in 1966 when the television networks provided the Republican party with a half-hour slot. Senator Everett Dirksen (Republican, Illinois) and Representative Gerald R. Ford (Republican, Michigan) delivered the first opposition response.
- By 1976 the television networks were providing a slot for the opposition party almost immediately after the Address.

THE STATE OF THE UNION

President George W. Bush's Eulogy for President Ronald Reagan

The National Cathedral
Washington, D.C.

12:09 P.M. EDT

THE PRESIDENT: Mrs. Reagan, Patti, Michael, and Ron; members of the Reagan family; distinguished guests, including our Presidents and First Ladies; Reverend Danforth; fellow citizens:

We lost Ronald Reagan only days ago, but we have missed him for a long time. We have missed his kindly presence, that reassuring voice, and the happy ending we had wished for him. It has been ten years since he said his own farewell; yet it is still very sad and hard to let him go. Ronald Reagan belongs to the ages now, but we preferred it when he belonged to us.

In a life of good fortune, he valued above all the gracious gift of his wife, Nancy. During his career, Ronald Reagan passed through a thousand crowded places; but there was only one person, he said, who could make him lonely by just leaving the room.

America honors you, Nancy, for the loyalty and love you gave this man on a wonderful journey, and to that journey's end. Today, our whole nation grieves with you and your family.

When the sun sets tonight off the coast of California, and we lay to rest our 40th President, a great American story will close. The second son of Nell and Jack Reagan first knew the world as a place of open plains, quiet streets, gas-lit rooms, and carriages drawn by horse. If you could go back to the Dixon, Illinois of 1922, you'd find a boy of 11 reading adventure stories at the public library, or running with his brother, Neil, along Rock River, and coming home to a little house on Hennepin Avenue. That town was the kind of place you remember where you prayed side by side with your neighbors, and if things were going wrong for them, you prayed for them, and knew they'd pray for you if things went wrong for you.

The Reagan family would see its share of hardship, struggle and uncertainty. And out of that circumstance came a young man of steadiness, calm, and a cheerful confidence that life would bring good things. The qualities all of us have seen in Ronald Reagan were first spotted 70 and 80 years ago. As a lifeguard in Lowell Park, he was the protector keeping an eye out for trouble. As a sports announcer on the radio, he was the friendly voice that made you see the game as he did. As an actor, he was the handsome, all-American, good guy, which, in his case, required knowing his lines -- and being himself.

Along the way, certain convictions were formed and fixed in the man. Ronald Reagan believed that everything happened for a reason, and that we should strive to know and do the will of God. He believed that the gentleman always does the kindest thing. He believed that people were basically good, and had the right to be free. He believed that bigotry and prejudice were the worst things a person could be guilty of. He believed in the Golden Rule and in the power of prayer. He believed that America was not just a place in the world, but the hope of the world.

And he believed in taking a break now and then, because, as he said, there's nothing better for the inside of a man than the outside of a horse.

Ronald Reagan spent decades in the film industry and in politics, fields known, on occasion, to change a man. But not this man. From Dixon to Des Moines, to Hollywood to Sacramento, to Washington, D.C., all who met him remembered the same sincere, honest, upright fellow. Ronald Reagan's deepest beliefs never had much to do with fashion or convenience. His convictions were always politely stated, affably argued, and as firm and straight as the columns of this cathedral.

There came a point in Ronald Reagan's film career when people started seeing a future beyond the movies. The actor, Robert Cummings, recalled one occasion. "I was sitting around the set with all these people and we were listening to Ronnie, quite absorbed. I said, 'Ron, have you ever considered someday becoming President?' He said, 'President of what?' 'President of the United States,' I said. And he said, 'What's the matter, don't you like my acting either?'"

The clarity and intensity of Ronald Reagan's convictions led to speaking engagements around the country, and a new following he did not seek or expect. He often began his speeches by saying, "I'm going to talk about controversial things." And then he spoke of communist rulers as slave masters, of a government in Washington that had far overstepped its proper limits, of a time for choosing that was drawing near. In the space of a few years, he took ideas and principles that were mainly found in journals and books, and turned them into a broad, hopeful movement ready to govern.

As soon as Ronald Reagan became California's governor, observers saw a star in the West -- tanned, well-tailored, in command, and on his way. In the 1960s, his friend, Bill Buckley, wrote, "Reagan is indisputably a part of America, and he may become a part of American history."

Ronald Reagan's moment arrived in 1980. He came out ahead of some very good men, including one from Plains, and one from Houston. What followed was one of the decisive decades of the century, as the convictions that shaped the President began to shape the times.

He came to office with great hopes for America, and more than hopes -- like the President he had revered and once saw in person, Franklin Roosevelt, Ronald Reagan matched an optimistic temperament with bold, persistent action. President Reagan was optimistic about the great promise of economic reform, and he acted to restore the reward and spirit of enterprise. He was optimistic that a strong America could advance the peace, and he acted to build the strength that mission required. He was optimistic that liberty would thrive wherever it was planted, and he acted to defend liberty wherever it was threatened.

And Ronald Reagan believed in the power of truth in the conduct of world affairs. When he saw evil camped across the horizon, he called that evil by its name. There were no doubters in the prisons and gulags, where dissidents spread the news, tapping to each other in code what the American President had dared to say. There were no doubters in the shipyards and churches and secret labor meetings, where brave men and women began to hear the creaking and rumbling of a collapsing empire. And there were no doubters among those who swung hammers at the hated wall as the first and hardest blow had been struck by President Ronald Reagan.

The ideology he opposed throughout his political life insisted that history was moved by impersonal ties and unalterable fates. Ronald Reagan believed instead in the courage and triumph of free men. And we believe it, all the more, because we saw that courage in him.

As he showed what a President should be, he also showed us what a man should be. Ronald Reagan carried himself, even in the most powerful office, with a decency and attention to small kindnesses that also defined a good life. He was a courtly, gentle and considerate man, never known to slight or embarrass others. Many people across the country cherish letters he wrote in his own hand -- to family members on important occasions; to old friends dealing with sickness and loss; to strangers with questions about his days in Hollywood. A boy once wrote to him requesting federal assistance to help clean up his bedroom.

The President replied that, "unfortunately, funds are dangerously low." He continued, "I'm sure your mother was fully justified in proclaiming your room a disaster. Therefore, you are in an excellent position to launch another volunteer program in our nation. Congratulations."

Sure, our 40th President wore his title lightly, and it fit like a white Stetson. In the end, through his belief in our country and his love for our country, he became an enduring symbol of our country. We think of his steady stride, that tilt of a head and snap of a salute, the big-screen smile, and the glint in his Irish eyes when a story came to mind.

We think of a man advancing in years with the sweetness and sincerity of a Scout saying the Pledge. We think of that grave expression that sometimes came over his face, the seriousness of a man angered by injustice -- and frightened by nothing. We know, as he always said, that America's best days are ahead of us, but with Ronald Reagan's passing, some very fine days are behind us, and that is worth our tears.

Americans saw death approach Ronald Reagan twice, in a moment of violence, and then in the years of departing light. He met both with courage and grace. In these trials, he showed how a man so enchanted by life can be at peace with life's end.

And where does that strength come from? Where is that courage learned? It is the faith of a boy who read the Bible with his mom. It is the faith of a man lying in an operating room, who prayed for the one who shot him before he prayed for himself. It is the faith of a man with a fearful illness, who waited on the Lord to call him home.

Now, death has done all that death can do. And as Ronald Wilson Reagan goes his way, we are left with the joyful hope he shared. In his last years, he saw through a glass darkly. Now he sees his Savior face to face.

And we look to that fine day when we will see him again, all weariness gone, clear of mind, strong and sure, and smiling again, and the sorrow of his parting gone forever.

May God bless Ronald Reagan, and the country he loved.

RONALD REAGAN

THE STATE OF THE UNION